Contingent Creatures

WITHDRAWN

Contingent Creatures

A Reward Event Theory of Motivation and Value

CAROLYN R. MORILLO

LITTLEFIELD ADAMS BOOKS

LITTLEFIELD ADAMS BOOKS

Published in the United States of America
by Rowman & Littlefield Publishers, Inc.
4720 Boston Way, Lanham, Maryland 20706

3 Henrietta Street
London WC2E 8LU, England

British Cataloging in Publication Information Available

Library of Congress Cataloging-in-Publication Data

Morillo, Carolyn R.
Contingent creatures : a reward event theory of motivation and value /
Carolyn R. Morillo.
p. cm.
Includes bibliographical references and index.
1. Reward (Psychology) 2. Motivation (Psychology)
3. Reinforcement (Psychology) 4. Values. I. Title.
BF505.R48M67 1995 128'.4—dc20 95–11201 CIP

ISBN 0–8226–3040–0 (cloth : alk. paper)
ISBN 0–8226–3041–9 (pbk. : alk. paper)

Printed in the United States of America

℗™ The paper used in this publication meets the minimum requirements of
American National Standard for Information Sciences—Permanence of
Paper for Printed Library Materials, ANSI Z39.48–1964.

In memory of Norton Nelkin

Contents

CONTENTS

PREFACE

Since retiring from the University of New Orleans, I have moved to the Olympic Peninsula in Washington. I have gained mountains and the ocean but have lost daily personal contact with a unique philosophical community. I am therefore particularly indebted to those colleagues who through e-mail and snail mail packets have maintained our philosophical exchanges.

Norton Nelkin has over the years provided extensive written comments on my papers, including detailed comments on a final draft of this book. The steady challenge of his own distinctive theories has forced me to sharpen arguments and has demonstrated the benefits of an ongoing dialogue of mutual respect and determined disagreement.

Radu Bogdan really created our philosophical community through his organization and motivation of our Friday seminars. His own naturalizing projects have been an inspiration. He has also provided judicious e-mail nagging—"Get off the trails! Get back to work!"

Ed Johnson, who has been an exemplary chairman far longer than anyone should be saddled with that job, claimed to see a book in the making long before it was visible to me and has provided extensive suggestions, substantive and stylistic.

Dick Brandt has led the way in the development of a naturalistic theory of value rigorously grounded in empirical psychological data. In an ongoing correspondence, he has been generous with both encouragement and criticisms.

A number of others have provided forceful and helpful criticisms of my theories at our Friday seminars and at our annual state convention; these have included Robert Berman, Ronna Burger, Keith Butler, Graeme Forbes, Steve Giambronne, John Glenn, Harvey Green, Eric Mack, Mary Sirridge, and Jim Stone.

There is always a special debt to one's family. Centrally, and in terms of my own theory, my husband Marvin and our sons Stephen and John have been a source over the years of countless Reward Events. Marvin's lively intelligence and distinctive sensibility have moderated my tendency to get lost in the abstractions of high theory. Stephen and John have long since been on their own in pursuing academic careers but have been tolerant recipients of my progress reports, as well as patient providers of tips and emotional support for taming my computer. Along with their wives, Kim Milone and Andrea Atkin, they form an in-family community that is both intellectually stimulating and a delight to be around.

A late family member should be mentioned. Our quirky feline TM survived transplanting from New Orleans to Port Angeles and almost made it into her twentieth year. Like all cats, she had an instinctive ability to dwell for hours in pure pleasure without a single puritan qualm.

Finally, there is a special dedication, grounded in a darker side of my project. I have made use of scientific data that have been obtained from experiments on thousands of animals, who have been shocked, decorticated, folded, spindled, and mutilated. It is with humility and a bleak sense of inadequacy that I dedicate this book to all those animals.

Port Angeles, Washington
1995

ACKNOWLEDGMENTS

Material in chapter 1 has been drawn from my article, "Epistemic luck, naturalistic epistemology and the ecology of knowledge," *Philosophical Studies* 46 (1984) 109-129, © 1984 by D. Reidel Publishing Company. Reprinted by permission of Kluwer Academic Publishers, Spuiboulevard 50, PO Box 17, 3300 AA Dordrecht, The Netherlands.

Material in chapter 2 has been drawn from my article, "The reward event and motivation," *The Journal of Philosophy* 87 (1990) 169-186, © 1990 by The Journal of Philosophy, Inc., 709 Philosophy Hall, Columbia University, New York, NY 10027. Reprinted by permission of The Journal of Philosophy.

Material in chapter 2 has been drawn from my article, "Reward event systems: reconceptualizing the explanatory roles of motivation, desire and pleasure," *Philosophical Psychology* 5 (1992) 7-32, © 1992 by Journals Oxford Ltd. Reprinted by permission of Carfax Publishing Company, PO Box 25, Abingdon, Oxfordshire OX14 3UE, United Kingdom.

Gary Hardin used his professional book-designing skills to transform my files into book-ready form. I thank him for his skill and patience.

INTRODUCTION

What kind of creatures are we? Why do we act in the ways we do? Is there anything in our lives that has intrinsic value?

Philosophers have considered these questions for as long as our enterprise has existed. This book provides my answers to these questions. The term 'answers' may, however, suggest a misleading finality. I am offering a theory that is grounded in a combination of recent empirical developments in neuropsychology and of philosophical interpretations and analyses; both the empirical data and the analyses are provisional.

The overall perspective of the book is naturalistic. I believe the natural universe is fundamentally contingent in a way that blocks the kind of ultimate rational explanation that many have sought. Our best explanations for the ways of the universe are scientific explanations, and such explanations must finally end with the acknowledgment that the universe "just is." (See Morillo 1977a)

Within a universe that is contingent in that sense, there are more specific contingencies whose roles I shall stress: contingencies of the environment in our cognitive success and contingencies of associations in the development of specific motivations and specific sources of value. At the same time, some of these contingencies arise out of causal connections of the kind stressed by psychologists when they speak, for example, of the "contingencies of reinforcement."

Human beings are also contingent in the sense that they are one among many species of natural creatures that have evolved in the history of life on Earth. The record is not one of unidimensional progress culminating in "us"; it is instead the record of many opportunistic successes and of many more ultimate failures. I will not be providing arguments for this general naturalistic background; it is a framework I will take for granted as I focus on the more specific questions mentioned above.

The main themes of the book have arisen out of my earlier attempts (Morillo 1990, 1992) to develop the implications, for traditional philosophical theories of motivation, of a growing body of empirical evidence for the role of reward centers in the brain. I have used, and in this book shall continue to use, the fairly neutral term 'Reward Events' as a label for the key brain events, but I will argue that there are good reasons to interpret these events as instances of pleasure.

The Reward Event Theory that I develop—and that assigns a key role to Reward Events in both motivation and value—is thus a version of both psychological hedonism and value hedonism. It is, however, a revisionist version, shaped both by recent empirical evidence on the role of Reward Events and by my interpretation of pleasure as an intrinsic quality of experience. I hope to give these ancient theories, which are periodically proclaimed to have been refuted, a new hearing.

The main themes of the book can be summarized as follows:

Chapter 1, "Ecology and Affect in Naturalized Cognition," is a brief look at our cognitive equipment and skills. Philosophical theories of motivation and of value have too often assumed that cognition must play the decisive role in accounts of us as rational beings. I stress the role of the contingencies of a creature's environment (its ecology) in determining its cognitive success; this is part of a reliabilist, externalist theory of knowledge (which I do not develop in full here). I also summarize some of the empirical evidence for the causal influence, in cognition, of affect—understood as positive hedonic tone (pleasure).

Chapter 2, "Contingent Creatures as Reward Event Systems," is the empirical core of the book. Here, I summarize the neuropsychological evidence for the role of Reward Events in the brain and then argue that this evidence provides support for my Reward Event Theory of motivation. The key claim of the theory is that, in creatures who are Reward Event Systems, only Reward Events are intrinsically motivating. Reward Events are the essential causal anchor for any other motivations that may be focused on more traditional external objects, such as food (or the eating of food), sex partner (or the mating with same), or even such sophisticated human goals as saving the whales or cornering the market in silver. Such externally focused activities (or the thought of such activities) will be motivating if and only if they periodically connect with (are reinforced by) Reward Events in the brain. In this sense, only Reward Events are desired for their own sake, though such events are usually not the intentional object of our conscious motivations. I use this theory to criticize some standard arguments against psychological egoism. I also begin my arguments for an interpretation of Reward Events as pleasure events and for pleasure as the quality of positive hedonic tone. I argue that this nonoperational, nonfunctional conception of pleasure has theoretical advantages in providing explanations for phenomena that are otherwise merely relabeled.

Chapter 3, "Psychological Hedonism as an Empirical Theory," continues the arguments for my conceptualization of pleasure. As an intrinsic quality, pleasure has only contingent connections with either cognition or motivation. I sketch some psychologies in which the standard connections are severed. I also argue that my conceptualization has the advantage of making narrow psychological hedonism (a claim about what kinds of experiences of our own we are ultimately motivated to pursue) an empirical theory.

Chapter 4, "Naturalizing Value," presents my naturalistic theory of intrinsic value. (Throughout the book, I stress that I am presenting only a half theory; a full theory would include roles for intrinsically negative hedonic tone, the intrinsically bad.) I argue that certain naturalistic constraints and constraints of plausibility support the view that only pleasure is intrinsically good. I also give further arguments for my conceptualization of pleasure and argue against theories that interpret pleasure in terms of a relational property. Finally, I present some initial arguments for the surprising claim that intrinsic value—the intrinsically good—is nevertheless not normative.

Chapter 5, "Summing Up the Good Life," develops the implications of the Reward Event Theory (RET) of value for the question,: What makes a life good for the creature whose life it is? I defend the possibility of a coherent conception of maximizing pleasure through a lifetime; I also point out some of the difficulties for preference theories of value in providing any plausible conception of such maximization. I then defend RET's theory of the good life, as the maximization of pleasure, against some standard philosophical arguments that appeal to intuitions about Experience Machines and about what we really want. I use RET's theory of motivation to explain these intuitions, to defuse their argumentative force, and to focus on the ideology of value. What I stress is that the intrinsically good (pleasure) is the same in all creatures, human or nonhuman, who are Reward Event Systems, and that, in this sense, all good lives are the same. On the other hand, the intrinsically good (pleasure) is contingently connected with very different experiences and activities, both in different creatures and in the same creature over time; in this sense, what is good for one individual may not be good for another.

Chapter 6, "Reasons, Norms, Cognition, and Affect," returns to the issue of the normative. I focus primarily on theories of reasons or rationality and argue that these theories often make assumptions about the role of cognitive aspects of our psychology (e.g., beliefs and desires, as states with intentional content) that lead them to overlook the role of noncognitive affect, and specifically of hedonic tone. The result is that the perennially popular project of building ethical theory on a theory of rationality is likely to be empirically suspect. I then reply to the charge that my theory commits the "naturalistic fallacy"; I emphasize again that I am not offering a theory of ethics but only a theory of nonmoral intrinsic value.

Chapter 7, "Hedonism, Ideology, and Temperament," acknowledges current social pressures that are likely to make it difficult to defend hedonism. I then briefly hand-wave toward the issue of the ontological status of Reward Events; for example, whether they are epiphenomenal to brain events. Finally, I note why, in a certain sense, I am not temperamentally suited to hedonism as that theory is often understood. I have argued myself into the theory and have been surprised at where I have come out. My own intuitions are only now beginning to fit comfortably with my arguments, so that I can defend the Reward Event Theory as my current best answer to questions about motivation and value.

That is the book in outline. I must now leave my Reward Event Theory to the contingencies of evidence and argument.

1

ECOLOGY AND AFFECT
IN NATURALIZED COGNITION

While I will throughout this book be stressing noncognitive aspects of our psychology, this is not intended to suggest that cognition is unimportant. That would make no sense either from an evolutionary, psychological, or philosophical perspective. Any living creature must respond differentially to its environment, welcoming the helpful and rejecting the harmful. Such responses must be guided by reliable information about the world. Thus, natural creatures have evolved a variety of mechanisms and methods for gaining such information, from sense organs to sophisticated central processing.

Just where and how in this evolution there came on the scene creatures to whom we should ascribe mental representations, beliefs, desires, and full-scale intentionality (the ability to think *about* the world and even about nonexistent objects) has been a central question for the philosophy of mind. The issue of how to naturalize these difficult concepts—and how to model them in a clearly physical system—is also central to much of the work in artificial intelligence and the cognitive sciences and even structures the debate as to whether such folk psychological concepts will eventually be eliminated in a fully scientific psychology or its successor science.

Whatever the outcome of these debates, it remains clear that any creature that manages to survive (and reproduce) must be able to gain

1

and to utilize relevant information about its world. If this ability is thought of, generically, as a creature's *cognitive* skills, it is understandable that cognition could come to be seen as encompassing all of psychology and that creatures would be seen as information-processing systems of varying degrees of sophistication.

These labels can be misleading, however. In the history of psychology, cognition has often been contrasted with conation and affect. These categories point to differences that should not be obscured. In addition, these distinctions continue to be exploited in a large body of empirical psychological research.

A creature needs *relevant* information and must welcome the helpful and reject the harmful. This already points beyond the mere gathering of any and all information or the simple generation of sundry true beliefs. This chapter explores some constraints on the ability of natural creatures to gain information about *biologically relevant* properties of the environment; I also speculate on a possible mechanism for solving at least some of the problems of relevance. Further issues having to do with motivation, with welcoming and rejecting, and with the *valencing* of information will be dealt with in subsequent chapters.

I will defend two central claims. First, the ability to gain information about biologically relevant properties cannot be *guaranteed* through lawful connections (causal or otherwise) between the organism and those properties. Instead, the solution that is characteristic of evolved equipment depends crucially on the creature operating in the right ecology. Thus, in any individual case, success depends not only on properly functioning equipment but also on the contingencies of the environment, that is, on a degree of luck.

Second, a large body of empirical psychological evidence supports the influence of *affect* (a term ranging from specific emotions to moods) on cognitive processes. Affective states have been seen as, variously, providing information about internal states of the organism, focusing attention on relevant external states of affairs, disrupting the reliability of beliefs formed under the influence of affect, providing a vital mechanism for organizing memory and for providing relevance, and so on.

If affect is seen as disrupting reliable cognition, it may seem most plausible to think of it as noncognitive, as a rival and distinct type of psychological state. On the other hand, if affect is seen as contributing to cognitive success, it may come to be seen as just another part of our overall cognitive equipment. I will argue that affective states— even if partially constituted (as in some emotions) by a paradigmatically cognitive state such as a belief that *p* or the representing of the information that *p*—*essentially involve intrinsic qualities of positive or negative hedonic tone*, and that this involvement is not true for any belief state in itself. There is evidence for the causal influence of hedonic qualities on our cognitive processing, and thus an adequate understanding of cognition (of the gaining and utilizing of information) requires an understanding of the role of these noncognitive states. In addition, I later argue for a central causal role for positive and negative hedonic tone in learning (e.g., in classical and operant conditioning) and in the shaping of specific motivations and subsequent behavior. Thus, cognitive psychology, seen as the whole of psychology, either omits key causal pieces needed for understanding complex organisms or so extends the term 'cognition' that important distinctions are obscured.

ECOLOGY AND COGNITION

If our sense organs and our ways of knowing have evolved, what constraints does that put on what we can expect of this equipment? I will argue that a naturalistic perspective, emphasizing ecological constraints, undercuts many traditional assumptions about the conditions necessary for knowledge. We should either reconstruct the traditional conception or conclude that knowledge in this traditional sense does not matter that much.

If we ordinarily contrast knowledge with lucky guesses or accidentally true beliefs, this contrast suggests that we take knowledge to exclude luck and accident. This initial suggestion has been reinforced by discussions of the Gettier problems and the Lottery Paradox (see Dretske 1981, 96-102; Pollock 1986, 180-193), in which solutions have tended to take the view that even very high probabilities or very strong justifications are not enough if these still allow even the occasional bad luck or the occasional unfortunate accident (i.e., false belief). Thus, many analyses of knowledge have required that it be *not at all* accidental that one is right, or that there be some causal, counterfactual, or other appropriate *nomological* connection between the knower and the known that would carry a conditional probability of one, thus reducing any element of luck or accident to zero.

Because that which is a matter of luck or accident is not within our control, we might suppose that the *denial* of any luck or accident in knowledge would be particularly characteristic of internalist theories that require full awareness of the grounds of knowledge and stress concepts of justification (or reasonable belief) that allow us to control whether our beliefs are justified (or reasonable). If we combine this denial with the elimination of bad luck (false beliefs), it all begins to sound quite Cartesian. But instead we find that the "no accident," nomological analyses are characteristically externalist,[1] naturalistic, and anti-Cartesian.

This is a surprising combination. An externalist, naturalistic epistemology, of the kind I would defend, should acknowledge that there is a significant element of luck in knowledge, which no nomological connections can overcome. Externalism does provide a reasonable way to demystify skeptical ghosts, so to this degree, the anti-Cartesian claims of such views are well taken. Naturalism should teach us, however, that there are no guarantees against vulnerability and that any attempt to erect them, internal or external, is one more doomed Cartesian enterprise.

My focus will be restricted primarily to *de re* perceptual beliefs. If a naturalistic theory cannot handle these properly, it is in trouble.

The basic outline of my argument is simple.[2] I start with the premise that truth is a central virtue of a single belief.[3] Having reasonably correct information about the world is indispensable for biological success. If this is so, then when we call a true belief unreasonable or unjustified or not really knowledge, what is being evaluated is not that belief as such. After all, if the belief is true, how can *it* be any better? The commonplace reply is that we are evaluating the *method* used for arriving at the belief.

What, then, are the virtues of a method? If one accepts truth as a central epistemic value, a partial reply is: some degree of reliability in the production of truth. Externalist, naturalistic epistemologies characteristically replace method (a fairly internalist notion) with mechanism. And it is at this point that the nomological connections are inserted, whether expressed in causal, informational, or counterfactual terms. The assumption seems to be that these strong connections are the key to making us knowers, rather than mere true believers.[4] And yet how odd this is from a naturalistic point of view. Surely any plausible naturalism must see us and our mechanisms for knowing as having evolved through natural selection. And when has evolution ever produced any infallible, fail-safe mechanisms, perceptual or otherwise? Equipment alone does not make for biological (or epistemic) success; it has to be equipment in the right context. It is not neurology that makes us knowers, but neurology *plus* ecology. The key connection is between an organism (knower) and the biologically (epistemologically) relevant properties of its environment—and that connection is not and never could be nomological.

These claims can be illustrated by two well-known examples, one biological and the other philosophical. The former concerns the frog's ability to detect and zap bugs; the latter has to do with the impact of "faux barns" (such as convincing movie facades) on our ability to know by looking that one sees a barn in a field.

A classic source for a description of our biological example is the much-cited article by Lettvin et al. (1959, 1951; quoted in Dretske 1981, 240):

> Such a fiber responds best when a dark object, smaller than receptive field, enters that field, stops, and moves about intermittently thereafter. The response is not affected if the lighting changes or if the background (say a picture of grass and flowers) is moving, and is not there if only the background, moving or still, is in the field. Could one better describe a *system for detecting an accessible bug?*

Consider next a commentary on this example by Dretske (1981):

> It seems clear that certain neurons are labeled "bug detectors", not simply because a moving bug *causes* them to fire, but because, in the frog's natural habitat, *only* a moving bug (or relevant equivalent stimulus) causes them to fire. It is this *informational* relationship to the stimulus that entitles the neural cell to be called a *detector* of bugs. (34-35)

This is a characteristic claim that knowledge requires some nomically based, "no equivocation" reliability (a claim Dretske has subsequently modified). The difficulty with such a claim, when placed in a naturalistic context, is apparent. Is it the case—could it possibly be the case—that in the frog's natural habitat *only* a moving bug could cause the relevant neurons to fire? And what besides a bug could be a *biologically* "relevant equivalent stimulus"? Surely in the life of any single frog, and even more in the evolutionary history of the species, there would be some false allures when some small nonedible object duplicated the motion of a bug. Evolution, and even individual survival, do not require infallibility, though some false allures (or alarms) can be fatal.

Consider again the quotation from Lettvin et al.: "a dark object, smaller than a receptive field, enters that field, stops, and moves about intermittently thereafter." For convenience, let us use the abbreviation SEMO (for small erratically moving object). One can be sure, given standard laboratory techniques, that many frogs in Lettvin's lab reacted to (zapped) SEMOs that were not bugs. Admittedly, Lettvin's lab is not the environment in which frogs evolved their detecting equipment, but times and environments change.

If we think seriously about the frog case, I think it supports the following claims:

1. Of course frogs evolved bug-detecting equipment and not just SEMO-detecting equipment; only the former has any *biological* point and would figure in any explanation of the evolution of such equipment.
2. Whether the frog's equipment actually functions as bug-detectors depends not only on the equipment but also on the habitat.
3. In general, whether organisms are able to detect biologically relevant properties depends not only on neurology but also on ecology.
4. Neurology *may* be law-governed, and responses to SEMOs *may* also be law-governed, but the biologically relevant connections between organism and environment (e.g., frog to bug), because they depend on an ecology that can and does change through accident (or whim of an experimenter), are *never* law-governed.
5. For a naturalistic theory, biologically relevant properties and connections are the prototype of epistemologically relevant properties and connections, so the latter are as unlikely to be law-governed, "nomic", or absolute as the former. In brief, lucky frogs zap bugs, unlucky frogs contribute to scientific publications, and frogs *are* good bug-detectors.

Consider next a human case—Goldman's well-known faux barn example (1976)—which raises the issue of how someone's ability to know by looking that he sees a barn in a field is affected by the existence of papier-mâché facsimiles of barns that are indistinguishable from real barns by those looking while driving by. This is the issue of relevant alternatives, which must be faced by any naturalistic theory of knowledge. As Goldman has stated:

> In the spirit of naturalistic epistemology, I am trying to fashion an account of knowing that focuses on more primitive and pervasive aspects of cognitive life, in connection with which, I believe, the term 'know' gets its application. A fundamental facet of animate life, both human and infra-human, is telling things apart, distinguishing predator from prey, for example, or a protective habitat from a threatening one. The concept of knowledge has its roots in this kind of cognitive activity. (791)

Compare the faux-barn case with Dretske's 1981 discussion of lottery cases, which he took to provide intuitive and theoretical support for his claim that knowledge requires nomically based, *zero* equivocation.

Dretske asks us to consider drawing a ball at random from an urn:

> You draw a ball from an urn containing 90 pink balls (P), 3 yellow balls (Y), 3 blue balls (B), and 4 green balls (G). Given that you are drawing a ball at random from an urn with this relative distribution of colored balls, the probability of drawing a pink ball is 0.9. . . . Suppose K receives a message containing the information that you randomly drew a ball from an urn having this distribution of colored balls. . . . Assuming that you do, in fact, draw a pink ball, does K *know* that you did? *Can* he know that you did? . . . It seems clear to me that he does *not* know it. . . . And there is no significant change in this situation if we increase the relative proportion of pink balls. As long as the information is absent, as it always will be when there are any other colored balls in the urn, knowledge is impossible. (94-95)

Let us apply Dretske's analysis to Goldman's faux-barn case. If looking while driving by is a way of sampling from the *world* urn, then a facsimile in Sweden is an "other colored ball," and knowledge that one is seeing a barn in Wisconsin is impossible. Should we then restrict the context for relevant alternatives to Wisconsin (or to *this* field)? Suppose our urn is a very large urn and that in fact all the "other colored balls" are in a part very far from where you are drawing, though you and others don't know this. Why can we not, in considering such a case, restrict the context and say that we do *know* you will draw or have drawn a pink ball?

The key point is that we never can establish zero equivocation for any signal as such unless we do so relative to a restricted context that rules out a priori any ringers. This quite trivializes, however, any zero-equivocation requirement.

We can put this in a slightly different way. If we are allowed to restrict the context to one in which all looks-like-a-barn objects *are* barns, then of course when our driver selects a looks-like-a-barn, he gets a barn. In the same way, if we can restrict the context to that section of the urn in which all balls are pink, then of course we'll get a pink ball. The *reductio* of this way of restricting context is that it can eventually collapse into a context of "this barn" or "this pink ball," at which point any distinction between knowledge and true belief also collapses.

Remember my earlier premise that in deciding whether a true belief is knowledge, we are not evaluating the belief as such but the method used to arrive at the belief. We can now draw the conclusion that any attempt to characterize the method of knowing as using signals only in those contexts in which they in fact *always* lead to true beliefs is at best a trivial and question-begging absolutism.

Goldman makes a further important point:

> Suppose F is the property of being a dog. Can we say that *b's-being-a-dog* is a cause of certain light waves being reflected? This is very dubious. It is the molecular properties of the surface of the animal that are causally responsible for this transmission of light, and hence for the percept.
>
> One might say that, even if the percept needn't be (perceptually) caused by *b*'s-having-*F*, it must at least be caused by microstructural properties of F that *ensure* *b*'s-having-*F*. As the dog example again illustrates, however, this is too strong. The surface properties of the dog that reflect the light waves do not *ensure* that the object is a dog, either *logically or nomologically*. . . . (785, my final emphasis)

We can generalize Goldman's point as follows: What we know about the structure and operation of sense organs indicates that they are nomologically responsive to microstructural properties of objects having to do with reflection of light and sound, chemical composition, etc. These properties as such are usually not biologically relevant. Nevertheless, sense organs have evolved because these various microstructural properties were fairly constantly (though surely not invariably) correlated with such important properties as "being a food object" or "being a predator." To illustrate with a nonvisual example, many male moths have sense organs that are extraordinarily sensitive to specific chemicals. Biologically, this is not because they are fascinated by that chemical but because that chemical is (or has been) characteristically correlated with "available female moth," and that *is* fascinating. This is not, however, and could not be a nomological connection. Indeed, it has been systematically violated by Evil Demon Experimenters who have attracted moths with the chemical *alone.*

Thus, there can always be equivocation with respect to relevant properties at the source (the distal object of perception). And if there is not—if context or habitat is remarkably stable—this stability is not due to the workings of any law or, usually, to any control by the organism. It is a matter of luck or accident.

This conclusion holds even if our sensory representations are due to a summation of different signals over time. This may well have been the best machinery for getting us correlated with biologically relevant properties, but it is still only correlation. It is one of the virtues of Goldman's article that he shows so clearly the connection between skepticism and alternatives at the source that are *perceptually* equivalent but not *biologically* or *epistemologically* equivalent.

It is likely that an organism (such as we are) that has developed flexibility, learning skills, and the ability to cross-check signals from many sources will over the long-haul be much less vulnerable to ringer objects. It is not in the human condition, however, (or the condition of any natural organism) to eliminate all epistemological vulnerability, even when we are operating at our best.

Some kinds of luck or accidents are, of course, quite compatible with an absolutist theory of knowledge. If, on such a view, knowledge is grounded in mechanisms providing nomic dependencies between object and knower, it does not matter at all how accidental the *origins* of such a mechanism happen to be. To illustrate, if a mixer filled with camera parts tumbled them about and quite by accident brought together parts that formed a perfectly good, working camera that gave lawfully reliable pictures, it would not impugn the reliability of the camera at all to point out this strange and unlikely origin. It's how it actually works that matters, not how it came about.

On any naturalistic theory, the same must be true for our mechanisms for knowing. Certainly no such theory would want to be committed to the view that the reliability of such mechanisms depends on their being *designed* to perform the way they do. The undoubted fact that our mechanisms have evolved may seem to make our case quite different from the chance-camera, but many contemporary interpretations of the course of evolution emphasize how many chance factors have influenced that course, as natural selection has operated on whatever material happened to be available in whatever environment happened to prevail and thus by fits and starts, with many blind alleys and dead ends, produced the swarms of odd and always, to a degree, Rube Goldberg creatures.[5]

My central claims do not depend on the fact that our various mechanisms are only generally reliable and are of course subject to breakdown. Even if it is in a sense accidental that a mechanism happens to be working correctly when put to use, this too need not matter to an absolutist theory. Nevertheless, to the degree that classifying a true belief as knowledge requires evaluation of the method or mechanism for producing the belief, a less-than-reliable mechanism may begin to undercut the epistemological significance of the nomic dependencies when they occur. A camera that works only one time out of a hundred may indeed make a fine picture that one time, but it is not what you would want to take on a long trip.

The heart of the matter as far as luck or accident goes is the role of stability of context, normalcy of environment, fixity of relevant alternatives in ensuring a proper fit between mechanisms (even ones that are mechanically infallible) and *relevant* properties. With sense organs that are tuned to physical properties that are only correlated with those relevant properties we claim to know, there is the ineliminable possibility of *perceptual* equivalents that are not *biological* or *epistemological* equivalents.

What all this comes down to, in a positive sense, is that for *de re* perceptual beliefs, S knows that *s* is *F* if, roughly, (1) S's belief that *s* is *F* was brought about by a reasonably reliable mechanism (not too many breakdowns between sense organs and the physical properties to which they respond), (2) it was brought about in a reasonably stable environment (not too many ringer perceptual equivalents), and (3) S was lucky enough this time to have avoided the breakdowns and the ringers. I doubt that anything more rigorous than this is realistic.

One can, of course, lessen one's reliance on luck to a considerable degree (sensory cross-checking, and so on), but too much of that sort of thing is scarcely compatible with getting on with the business of life. Knowing is like living with a camel. As nomadic tribes have discovered, they can be very useful on tough journeys, but they are never really tame and may yet spit in your eye.

This very brief defense of a reliabilist theory of knowledge is unlikely to satisfy critics of such theories. They will be even less convinced if one extends (as I would) reliabilism (as a form of externalism) to the issue of *justification*. While there are indeed technical difficulties in specifying the circumstances within which one is to assess the reliability of a method or mechanism (see Pollock 1986, 116-121), what I would stress is that from any naturalistic perspective, the point of reasoning, evidence, or justification is to provide a basis for believing *p* that is other than, but reliably correlated with, the state of affairs expressed by *p*. The only method not of this sort would be a direct access to that state of affairs that guarantees truth.

Defenders of justification internalism often insist on the normative role of justification and argue that we should be able to apply the concept of justification even to a brain in a vat, so that we could distinguish between reasonable and unreasonable epistemic behavior by a brain whose beliefs are uniformly unreliable (see Cohen 1984; Pollock 1986).

I confess I am not very concerned with whether the beliefs of a brain in a vat are justified in a sense that carries an implication of commendation or criticism of the poor brain. She (it?) has done all she can do, and on any theory that ties praise or blame exclusively to that which is within our control, she should not be blamed if things go wrong.

I am interested in the results of methods—a consequentialist stance. There is no deep point to being justified for its own sake (like having a pure moral will). The point of cognitive equipment is to help us to cope, usually by producing true beliefs. Certainly this role in coping should be the naturalistic story of perceptual equipment. One cannot rule out the possibility, in special circumstances, of some belief-producing mechanisms/methods contributing to survival/reproduction because they produce false beliefs—if, for example, the beliefs are not about states of the world of direct relevance to survival (Is this a predator?), and if the false beliefs produce psychic comfort or action or something that does contribute to survival/reproduction. Nature need not require epistemic purity all the way up, and whether we should require it is a complex normative issue I will not deal with here.[6]

The conclusion is that the ineliminable role of context—of the ecology of a creature in determining its overall success or failure—applies equally to epistemic success or failure. Whether a creature knows (in the sense of gaining relevant information), or flourishes in some broader sense, is subject to contingencies not within the creature's control, and is thus a matter of luck. Sometimes it takes only a little bit of luck—say, the continuation of a long-standing and well-established stability of context—and sophisticated cognitive equipment (such as ours) is very effective at adapting swiftly to environmental changes, but this may not always be enough to save us.[7]

Acknowledging the role of the luck of context is a first step away from a view of creatures (and particularly ourselves) as exclusively systems of *internal cognitive control*; this is not an accurate picture even when the tasks to be performed are cognitive. Indeed, as I will next argue, our cognition is subject not only to ecological constraints but also to causal influences from the affective dimensions of our psychology.

AFFECT AND COGNITION

In psychology, the term 'affect' has been used to cover a wide range of phenomena. According to one psychologist, the terms 'affect' and 'mood' are often used synonomously (Thayer 1989, 14). Equally common is the equation of affect with emotion (see the articles in Stein et al. 1990).

Much of the theoretical debate, within both psychology and philosophy, has been over the proper analysis or characterization of emotions (or moods, or affect). As de Sousa (1987) has observed, different theories "have variously taken feeling, behavior, physiology, cognition, will, evolution, or social context to offer the privileged perspective or the defining element," and he then comments that "the correct theory will have to avoid their partiality but will have learned from all of them" (22). If affect, or emotion, or mood is such a multi-faceted phenomenon, and if important claims are made about the causal role of affect, we need to be clear just which facets are playing which causal roles.

What I wish to emphasize in the following brief discussion of the role of affect in cognition is the distinction between cognition and a key, noncognitive dimension of affect. Making the distinction requires regimenting the concept of cognition, which itself can be interpreted as a multifaceted phenomenon, sometimes encompassing all dimensions of a creature's psychology, thus equating psychology with cognitive psychology.

A reasonable compromise, suggested by the tendency of cognitive psychology to see creatures as content-driven systems, is to interpret the term 'cognitive' as standing for any psychological state with representative or intentional content. This would include both beliefs (that p) and desires (that p), and thus is a departure from older usage, which equated cognition with belief and with thinking processes involving relations among beliefs, but which distinguished cognition from both emotion and conation.

Many psychological and philosophical theories of emotion or affect emphasize the cognitive dimensions, those aspects with intentional content, as in theories that argue that the various emotions are constituted by appropriate combinations of belief and desire. On the other hand, many psychological theories of emotion, mood, or affect postulate at least two different noncognitive dimensions—hedonic affect (both positive and negative) and arousal.

There is evidence that arousal and hedonic affect are distinct dimensions of subjective experience and may have distinct neural bases (Heller 1990). Thus, while I shall hereafter be emphasizing hedonic affect, it is likely that the complete causal story will include a number of noncognitive psychological states, that is, states without intentional content. (Thayer's biopsychological theory of moods [1989] distinguishes, for example, between energetic and tense arousal.)

I should also emphasize that I will develop a theory of positive hedonic affect or pleasure (and by implication of pain) that is often at odds with the theories of psychologists and of many philosophers. Specifically, I will argue that positive and negative hedonic tone are intrinsic qualities of experience, and that these qualities are causally connected with, but should not be defined in terms of, any cognitive or motivational states.

This is the basis for my disagreements with Armon-Jones (1991), who makes an excellent case for including in the domain of affect, not only those emotions conceptually requiring objects and that have been taken as paradigmatic by many recent philosophical studies of the emotions, but also emotions able to exist without objects. Also included are feeling states, such as moods, which characteristically can be free-floating or objectless. Armon-Jones's characterization of affect seems close to my own:

> The concept of affect is, I propose, primarily the concept of a feeling state. By this I mean that it is felt, occurrent states that provide those central or paradigm instances of affect which we use to explain the meaning of the term 'affect,' and from which the concept of affect derives its intelligibility. (4)

She also speaks of the "*intrinsic* identifying qualities" (9, my emphasis) of such feeling states. She insists, however, that her view of emotions (and moods) is a cognitive view. As she notes, traditionally the term 'cognitive' has been linked to epistemic attitudes such as knowledge and belief, "which entail a truth commitment" (12), and she argues against theories of emotion (or affect) that link it essentially with these sorts of cognitive states. But she also notes that contemporary psychologists use the term 'cognitive' more broadly, to cover "any mental process involving conceptualization—the organization of experience under concepts of some kind" (12), or as I have put it, to cover any psychological state with representative or intentional content. In this broader sense, Armon-Jones argues, the feelings with which she is concerned are not sensations (as I would agree), nor are they "raw feels" (a somewhat pejorative term for a psychological state with no intentional content, which might better be called pure feeling); they are instead intentional states involving an adverbial conceptualization of such sundry objects as "depressing," "frightful," "joyous," and so on, but involving no truth commitment (her primary disagreement with other cognitive views).

Such adverbial conceptualizations are complex attitudes toward, and thus relational properties of, sundry experiences, objects, and so on. The feelings Armon-Jones makes central to her theory are constituted by patterns of conceptualizations. By contrast, I will argue that the key feelings, which are indeed central to affect, are intrinsic qualities of experience that do not have any content—although they can, contingently, be associated with, and in that sense come to color, almost any intentional content.[8] The arguments will come later; for now I will briefly note some of the evidence for the causal influence of affect in cognition.

Thayer (1989) reviews the experimental literature connecting mood, memory, and other cognitive processes—a literature that leads him to conclude that "the nervous system appears to be organized in such a way as to make thoughts consistent in tone with mood states. . . ." (32).

With respect to memory, the research has built on the extensive work on state-dependent learning that "has frequently been demonstrated with animals as well as with humans (Overton, 1984)" [quoted in Thayer, 33]. As Thayer summarizes it:

> In such research, drugs that act on the central nervous system are employed to demonstrate that if learning occurs or attention given during a particular drug state, when the subjects are reintroduced to the same drug state later, they will have a better memory of what was learned than if recall is attempted in a nondrugged or a different drug state. This state-dependent memory retrieval has been demonstrated with such well-known drugs as alcohol and marijuana, as well as with a wide range of others, including various anesthetics, narcotics, anxiolytics, and stimulants. Even nicotine was recently employed to show state dependency (Peters & McGee, 1982). Early theorizing about this phenomenon centered on particular brain mechanisms, but more recent ideas have focused on the conditioning of stimulus contextual clues (cf. Tulving & Thompson, 1973) arising from the distinctive effects of various drugs (Overton, 1984). (33)

Thayer also notes that there is much research showing the influence of mood on a variety of other cognitive processes—that positive mood enhances creative processes (Isen, Daubman, and Nowicki 1987); that negative moods increase irrational thinking (Madigan and Bollenbach 1986); that thinking about the future is influenced by positive and negative moods (Alloy and Ahrens 1987; Brown 1984; Thayer 1987b; Wright and Bower 1981); that specific deficits related to mood disorders can be traced to problems in encoding and retrieving information congruent with the current mood and to activating memories associated with a particular mood (Johnson and Magaro 1987).

Additional evidence is accumulating from a more directly neurological perspective. In a recent volume on *Psychological and Biological Approaches to Emotion* (Stein et al. 1990), an article by Tucker et al. is summarized as follows:

> Tucker, Vannatta, and Rothlind discuss the role of the two hemispheres in regulating modes of cognition that structure emotional processes. In particular, they are interested in the unique functioning of the two hemispheres in regulating emotion. However, their chapter also focuses on the importance of primitive emotional processes in regulating higher order functioning like memory and attention. They review evidence suggesting

that the left and right hemisphere operate on different principles of neurophysiological self-regulation in regard to activation and arousal. The cognitive effects of these control mechanisms may help to explain how emotional states restrict or expand the breadth of attentional access to different types of information. These investigators also argue that in its regulation of memory functions, the neomamalian [*sic*] limbic system applies controls to human cognition, operating in parallel to more cortical, semantic representational functions. These limbic-system emotion controls involve special access routes for information that is hedonic or threatening. (xiv)

Rosenfield (1988) quotes from a study by Gloor et al. (1982) that corroborates this central role of the limbic system:

The observation that such responses ["memory experiences" elicited by electrical stimulation in the temporal lobes] can be more easily elicited by stimulating at the limbic than at the neocortical "end" of this system suggests that limbic action may be essential for bringing to a conscious level percepts elaborated by the temporal neocortex. One may conjecture that whatever we experience with our senses, particularly in the visual and auditory modalities, even after it has been elaborated as a percept in temporal neocortex, must ultimately be transmitted to limbic structures in order to assume experiential immediacy. *Attaching some affective or motivational significance to a percept may be the specific limbic contribution to this process. This may be the precondition for the percept to be consciously experienced or recalled and may imply that all consciously perceived events must assume some kind of affective dimension, if only ever so slight.* (Quoted in Rosenfield, 164-165; Rosenfield's emphasis)

Edelman, in his "neural Darwinism" theory of memory (1992; see 1987, 1989) also emphasizes the role of connections with the limbic system, which he calls the hedonic system (1992, 117) and which, in his theory, is the core of the organism's value system.

Damasio, in his recent book *Descartes' Error* (1994), argues at length for the vital role of emotion and feeling in reason and adaptive social behavior. His theory draws on his background as both a neurologist and a clinical psychologist and is based on his interpretation of the neurological bases of those sad "natural experiments"—human beings who have suffered brain damage. In particular, he describes in detail examples of the "Phineas Gage matrix" (named for a famous nineteenth century case). These unfortunate individuals often retain much of what is considered to constitute our rationality—knowledge, attention, and memory; language; and the ability to perform calculations or to deal with the logic of an abstract problem. What they lack is practical reason—the ability to apply their knowledge and skills to everyday decisions in ways that are either to their personal advantage and/or conform to common social standards, an ability they usually possessed prior to their illness or injury (unless the brain damage was congenital). In addition, they characteristically have lost their ability to experience emotions and feelings, though they do retain certain basic, short-term emotions such as rage or fear.

The neurological damage suffered by these individuals involves, in various combinations, the ventromedial prefrontal cortices, the somatosensory cortices in the right hemisphere, and the amygdala. Damasio summarizes his interpretation of this neurological evidence as follows:

> In short, there appears to be a collection of systems in the human brain consistently dedicated to the goal oriented thinking process we call reasoning, and to the response selection we call decision making, with a special emphasis on the personal and social domain. This same collection of systems is also involved in emotion and feeling, and is partly dedicated to processing body signals. (70)

Damasio also notes that there is a particular region in the human brain—the anterior cingulate cortex (a part of the limbic system)—where systems concerned with emotion/feeling, attention, and working memory closely interact. He speculates that this interaction is essential for what he calls the "energy" of external action and reasoning (see 71); patients with damage in this region exist in a state of "suspended animation," mental and external. Damasio also speaks of the "will" or "volition" having been preempted (73); I would suggest we could also speak of a loss of *motivation*.

Damasio develops an admittedly neo-Jamesian theory of the emotions. Primary emotions, which are innate and preorganized, have as their essences collections of bodily changes that have evolved as biological adaptations to appropriate triggering situations. These emotions "depend on limbic system circuitry, the amygdala and anterior cingulate being the prime players" (133). The rich variety of secondary emotions develops when primary emotions become paired in individual experience with types of situations, setting up what Damasio calls "acquired dispositional representations" (see 136-137).

Damasio distinguishes between emotions and the *feelings of emotions;* the emotion is primarily constituted by various bodily changes, while feelings are the "experience of those changes" (139). Note that this entails that for Damasio emotions are not essentially conscious phenomena, which no doubt helps him flank many contested issues when dealing with the emotions of nonhuman animals.

In all the above-cited literature, neurological evidence is being interpreted in terms of some theory, often admittedly speculative, about the relationships between neurological circuits and specific psychological phenomena. It is at this interface between neurology and psychology that many of the debates occur concerning the proper conceptualization of emotion or feeling or affect; two theories may seem to agree on the role of affect but may have very different interpretations of the phenomena.

To illustrate with Damasio's theory in relation to my own, while Damasio does argue for the role of emotions and feelings, he goes on to interpret these phenomena as essentially cognitive phenomena. He emphasizes the role of emotions in providing us with ongoing information about the state of our own bodies. I would agree that such information is vital and makes evolutionary sense; I am not offering a full-scale theory of emotions and would not contest that this informational role is an important *aspect* of emotions. It is Damasio's characterization of feelings with which I would disagree, if this characterization is intended to account for the role of feelings in motivation and evaluation.

According to Damasio, *"feelings are just as cognitive as any other perceptual image* . . . they are first and foremost about the body, that they offer us the cognition of our visceral and musculoskeletal state" (159). In addition to giving feelings and their associated emotions a key role in energizing thought and action, Damasio also claims that "by dint of juxtaposition, body images give to other images a *quality* of goodness or badness, of pleasure and pain" (159).

It is not clear why these images, and the information they provide about the body, have this distinctive quality as contrasted with other perceptual images. Just how did pleasure and pain, much less goodness and badness, suddenly enter the picture? Can information as such, even information about the state of our own bodies, play the motivational and evaluational roles claimed by Damasio? I will argue that these roles are played by positive and negative hedonic affect; these qualities have no representative content and are thus intrinsically noncognitive.

As I interpret this growing body of neuropsychological evidence, cognition—both in the narrower sense having to do with the gaining of information (true beliefs) and in the wider sense that includes any psychological state with representative content (as in the desire *that p*)—is causally influenced by noncognitive states. Any complete psychology must bring in such affective states; cognitive psychology is not the whole story, even with respect to cognition.

It is a further step, of course, to claim that it is hedonic affect, as an intrinsic quality of experience, that plays a key causal role. Some of the above-cited literature takes that further step, but the causal role of hedonic affect primarily comes to the fore in the context of discussions of motivation and of the role of reward or reinforcement in learning. It will be in that context, in the next chapter, that I make my case for a central causal role for hedonic states.

With respect to cognition, there is one final point to be made. Many recent theories, such as Damasio's, about the role of affect, moods, or emotions stress their positive contribution to the overall economy of creatures. In part, this is a reaction against an ancient tradition that sees the emotional as antithetical to and at odds with the rational. In part, it is a corollary of a naturalistic perspective that sees our emotional equipment as having evolved and as therefore likely to have played a functional role.

Since this book is written from a naturalistic perspective, I am sympathetic to such views. There is, however, an important distinction that should be kept in mind—a distinction between proximate and ultimate causes.

With respect to ultimate causes, we are seeking answers to the question: Why do creatures have emotions, moods, affective states, hedonic states? Here, an evolutionary account is most likely to give us the right kind of answer, and such an account may well stress a role for such states in solving cognitive problems, say of relevance and access (see de Sousa 1987; Thayer 1990). But the fact that a psychological state has evolved in part because it contributes to the solution of a cognitive problem does not mean that the state is itself a cognitive state. Evolution devises solutions to problems with whatever materials are at hand, and often those solutions are rather jerry-built.

In addition, a state can often play multiple roles, and the contribution of affect to cognition may be only one of its roles.

When we go on to ask questions about *proximate* causes, we need to distinguish among the different kinds of psychological states that may play such a role. No doubt some of these are cognitive states, in both the narrower and wider sense, but if affective states are among the proximate causes, then we must recognize a role for the noncognitive.

There is another advantage to distinguishing between ultimate and proximate causes. A state may have evolved as a solution to a cognitive problem, but such solutions are at best statistical and long-run. In any given instance, the state, as a proximate cause, may *not* make such a cognitive contribution and may even run counter to cognitive success. Indeed, if the ecology of a creature has changed significantly from that in which the state evolved, the state may on the whole be counterproductive.

I suspect that the truth about affect is somewhere between the extremes of its being totally functional and its being totally disruptive, as would fit the very mixed nature of the experimental evidence, some of which documents the ways in which affect contributes to cognitive success, and some of which documents the ways in which it disrupts cognition, though a distinction needs to be made between an immediate tactical contribution and a longer-term strategic role.

SUMMARY

This has been a very brief survey of cognition, primarily in the sense of the acquiring, accessing, and utilizing of information. I have stressed two main points. One is that even with respect to perception, the evolutionary solution to the acquisition of information is always statistical and relative to context (ecology); in any individual case, a creature must have not only good equipment but also a certain degree of luck. The second is that with respect to the problems of relevance in acquisition, recall, and utilization of information, one of the evolutionary solutions may make use of affective states that are not themselves cognitive, and that such states may in any individual case be disruptive.

Such a cognitive role for affect is important, but it is only part of the story. We need to turn next to the wider role of hedonic states in the motivation of those creatures who are what I shall call Reward Event Systems.

2

CONTINGENT CREATURES
AS REWARD EVENT SYSTEMS

Why do we act the way we do? This is often expressed as a question about our motivations or our wants or desires, particularly our ultimate motivations or desires. What do we want for its own sake? The question may take this form because of an assumed background model for the causes of action—the traditional belief/desire model—in which an appropriate belief/desire pair functions as both the *cause of* and a *rationalization for* an action by an agent.[1]

I will start with this framework; I will argue, however, that this standard causal model is seriously incomplete and is also misleading insofar as it leads us to assume that our everyday rationalizations of actions, which often give us our sense of understanding of ourselves and of others, thereby give us a correct causal account. I will also argue that any theory that is adequate to the empirical evidence will need to introduce considerable revisions in our everyday psychological concepts such as motive and desire.

Finally, I will introduce my Reward Event Theory and will argue that an *affective* concept, specifically pleasure, should play a key role in psychological explanation, distinct from the role of motivational or cognitive concepts. This makes the Reward Event Theory a form of hedonism, but it is a revisionist version since the theory has no place for anything that plays all the roles assigned to pleasure in most traditional forms of hedonism.

The explanatory role of pleasure will be developed in the context of recent discussions in neuropsychology of the role of brain reward mechanisms in behavior. I will argue for a nonoperational conception of pleasure as an intrinsic quality of experience that functions as an intrinsic reward. Since appeal to intrinsic qualities must rely on human introspection and extrapolated speculation about nonhuman subjects, this nonoperational conception goes against many explicit commitments in the scientific literature to more operational (or functional) definitions. I will argue that only a nonoperational conception of pleasure or reward can play a distinct, noncircular explanatory role.

The Reward Event Theory is a half theory, since I develop it only as a theory of pleasure and of positive motivation and value, though by implication it extends to a comparable theory of negative hedonic affect (a broader concept than "pain") and of negative motivation and value.

PSYCHOLOGICAL EGOISM AND ITS CRITICS

Consider an ancient and seemingly quite cynical answer to the question of ultimate motivations: The only thing any person is ever ultimately motivated to pursue is his or her own satisfaction. The usual label for this rather vaguely stated theory is psychological egoism.

There are often serious confusions in arguments for psychological egoism. In particular, someone may be confused about the difference between satisfaction in the sense of obtaining what one desires—in which sense it is trivially true that when we get what we want we are satisfied—versus a very different sense intended to focus on an aspect of experience—"felt satisfaction"— that is only contingently connected with getting what we want. I call such an internal event a *Reward Event*.[2]

Even if a defender of psychological egoism avoids that confusion, it is assumed by many philosophers that the theory has been decisively refuted by an argument often credited to Bishop Butler.

Here are two contemporary formulations of the argument. The first is from Rachels's discussion of psychological egoism (1986):

> There is a general lesson to be learned here, having to do with the nature of desire and its objects. If we have a positive attitude toward the attainment of some goal, then we may derive satisfaction from attaining it. But the *object* of our attitude is *the attaining of that goal;* and we must want to attain the goal *before* we can find satisfaction in it. We do not first desire some sort of "pleasurable consciousness" and then try to figure out how to achieve it. Rather, we desire all sorts of different things . . . and *because* [my emphasis] we desire those things we derive satisfaction from getting them. (59-60)

The second is from Feinberg's discussion of psychological egoism (1971):

> The very fact that he [Lincoln] did find satisfaction as a result of helping the pigs presupposes that he had a *preexisting* [my emphasis] desire for something other than his own happiness. . . . The *object* of Lincoln's desire was not pleasure; rather pleasure is the *consequence* of his preexisting desire for something else. . . . But if pleasure and happiness *presuppose* [my emphasis] desires for something other than pleasure and happiness, then the existence of pleasure and happiness in the experience of some people proves that those people have strong desires for something other than their own happiness—egoistic hedonism to the contrary. (p. 492)[3]

These arguments seem to be making the following claims:
1. In most (though not all) cases of human motivation, the ultimate object of the motivation or desire—what the agent wants for its own sake—is an external object or state of affairs, not an internal felt satisfaction (Reward Event).
2. There is a variety of such ultimate objects.
3. In many cases of such outwardly focused motivation, if the object is realized and the agent knows that it is, this may, as a contingent fact, cause a Reward Event in the agent, but in these cases the Reward Event will occur only if there is already a preexisting desire for an object other than that Reward Event; the desire is not causally dependent on the Reward Event.

Let us call this the *By-Product Theory.* According to this theory, human motivation is (at least in many cases):
1. outwardly focused,
2. pluralistic in its objects,
3. temporally and causally prior to any associated Reward Event.

It seems further to be assumed that once one has cleared up the logical and linguistic confusions in egoism, it will be obvious that this outward, pluralistic view of motivation is correct. If, however, a theory of human motivation is making empirical claims about how we work, can it be that easy? If one is sympathetic to the naturalistic enterprise, then one will expect that an understanding of motivation will need to be as responsive to scientific developments as our understanding of perception must be.

Slote recognized this when he argued in an early article (1964) that "psychological egoism may well have a basis in the empirical facts of human psychology" (531). The core of his case was as follows:

> Certain contemporary learning theorists, e.g., Hull and Skinner, have put forward behavioristic theories of the origin and functioning of human motives which posit a certain number of basically "selfish," unlearned primary drives or motives (like hunger, thirst, sleep, elimination, and sex), and explain all other, higher order, drives or motives as derived genetically from the primary ones via certain "laws of reinforcement," and further deny the "functional autonomy" of the higher-order desires or motives. . . .
>
> A given higher-order drive or motive is *not* functionally autonomous, i.e., is functionally dependent, if when we cut off all reinforcement of it by primary rewards (rewards of primary drives) and there are, in addition, both a sufficient number of "extinction trials" (occurrences of acts done from that higher-order motive which are not associated even indirectly, i.e., through other higher-order motives, with primary rewards) and a complete absence, during these extended trials, of primary rewards for any similar higher-order motives (to eliminate the possibility of generalization of primary rewards from motives other than that being extinguished), the higher-order drive or motive actually does extinguish, i.e., the person whose higher-order motive is being extinguished eventually, even if perhaps only very gradually, ceases to act from that higher-order motive. (531-532)

Compare this *Behavioristic Learning Theory of Motivation* (BLTM) to the By-Product Theory:

1. Since the background theory for BLTM is behaviorism, which countenances no internal psychological events,[4] the focus of motivation will be outward. The ultimate objects of motivation, however, will be much more severely restricted, to such things as food, water, sex-object, or perhaps eating food, drinking water, and copulating. Only unlearned, and in that sense primitive, objects will be on the list.
2. The theory is thus minimally pluralistic, unlike the wide-ranging pluralism of the By-Product Theory.

3. Since the primary drives or motives are unlearned, that is, genetically wired in, the theory seems to assume that these are temporally and causally prior to any primary rewards; some things (food, water, etc.) *are* rewards *because* we have primary drives for them.

A few comments are in order. First, for BLTM to be at all plausible, it must admit that at the level of everyday conscious experience, we are indeed focused on the great variety of objects that the By-Product Theory emphasizes; they are what we take to be our goals. The issue, however, is one of ultimate motives in a sense that explains why we act as we do. If we are not committed to the view that our everyday understanding of our motives is necessarily accurate, or provides an adequate explanation of our actions, we should perhaps expect to be surprised by what a theory of motivation tells us. What BLTM is saying is that while we are indeed *focused* on a great variety of goals, all of these are *anchored* in—derive their motivational force from—a few unlearned primary goals. And any defender of the By-Product Theory would have to admit that most of the goals of adults—the goals that are at issue—are learned. We are not born desiring to listen to Mozart or to corner the market in silver. That is why the claim that such learned goals never become functionally autonomous is the empirical heart of BLTM; it is a theory not merely about how we first come to learn new goals but about what *sustains* them as goals.

Second, despite their differences, BLTM and the By-Product Theory agree that desire or motivation is causally primary. In all (BLTM) or most (By-Product Theory) cases, a reward is a reward—is that which contingently satisfies us—*because* we desire it; we do not desire it because we have independently found it to be satisfying.

Third, both theories radically downplay the role of internal psychological Reward Events. BLTM, of course, officially denies there are any such events, or at least any that can or should be included in a scientific psychology. The By-Product Theory, while allowing that there are such events and that they do play a role in our psychology, must insist that with respect to much of adult motivation, such events are not causally primary but are merely contingent by-products of our desires for all sorts of things other than the internal events themselves. This claim is, after all, the heart of the case against psychological egoism.

I have stressed similarities between the By-Product Theory and BLTM in order to contrast them with the theory I will defend—the

Reward Event Theory (RET). RET (1) is anchored in *internal* Reward Events, (2) is, in a sense, strongly monistic, and (3) reverses the causal order, insisting that we intrinsically desire these Reward Events because we find them to be intrinsically satisfying; we do not find them to be intrinsically satisfying because we intrinsically desire them. RET is based on a developing neuropsychological model to which we must now turn.

THE REWARD EVENT THEORY OF MOTIVATION

RET is grounded empirically in a growing body of neuro-psychological evidence concerning the strongly rewarding and motivating effects of electrical stimulation of key areas of the brain (ESB), the psychological dominance of and/or addiction to certain drug experiences, and (most speculatively) the growing evidence for a common basis for all these phenomena in (probably) dopamine-based circuitry in the brain. Most of the ESB experiments have been on rats and other nonhuman animals, though there has been some human experimentation in which stimulation of these brain areas produced reports of a general sense of pleasure. The literature on drugs and on dopamine deals extensively with both animal and human cases (Engel et al. 1987; Wise 1982; Wise and Bozarth 1982, 1987; Wise and Rompre 1989).

The classic experiments were performed by Olds and Milner (1954), "in which they demonstrated that electrical stimulation of parts of the limbic system (septal area and diencephalic regions) of the rat had a powerful reenforcing effect in that it shaped the rat's lever-pressing behavior and made it respond at an extremely high rate" (Stellar and Stellar 1985, 18). Later experiments demonstrated that ESB "was a very strong motivated behavior, for rats took very strong foot shock in order to stimulate their own brains (Olds 1958)" (31-32).[5] Indeed, the stimulation has been shown "to have a suppressive effect on several pain-motivated withdrawal behaviors. . . . During lateral hypothalamic stimulation, rats fail to respond to strong ammonia-soaked swabs, which cause trigeminal pain in the olfactory membranes and they also show attenuated startle to intense auditory stimuli (Stellar, 1976)" (203). Other experiments demonstrated "the strong preference for ESB over food, even to the point of starvation

(Routtenberg & Lindy, 1965) . . ." (196). We might also note that early on "Heath (1964b) and his colleagues . . . extended these finding to humans and were able to elicit reports of hedonic experience upon brain stimulation in the same regions" (22).

While much of the work on ESB has focused on localizing and characterizing the precise neurochemical events involved, some researchers have been willing to speculate on the significance of the results for more general theories of motivation. Here are representative quotations:

> All motivated behaviors and associated hedonic processes share similar neurological mechanisms in the limbic systems and . . . all operate according to the same basic physiological and behavioral principles. (Stellar and Stellar 1985, 50)

> Students of brain stimulation reward generally share the conviction that this phenomenon is not merely a laboratory artifact, but rather represents the central activation of an endogenous reward system—a system that evolved to serve some natural reward or rewards like food for hungry animals, water for thirsty animals, or copulation for sexually receptive animals. (Wise and Rompre 1989, 219)

> [ESB] is commonly viewed as an artificial activation of the brain's normal positive reinforcement mechanisms and as such can be used as a model of goal-directed or reinforced behavior. . . . (Porrino 1987, 51)

Such claims are by no means a consensus, and the above-quoted researchers hedge their claims with cautions and qualifications. As discussion proceeds, I will note the kinds of contrary evidence motivating such cautions. For now, I will outline the positive commitments of RET and the conceptual revisions the theory requires.

One assumption of RET is that all the various cases documented in the research involve kinds of brain events that are sufficiently similar to constitute a theoretically interesting "natural kind," which I call the Reward Event. The other assumption is that all other natural rewards (e.g., food, water, sex) are rewarding because of appropriate connections with instances of the Reward Event, and that all learned rewards, motivations, or desires are functionally dependent on (i.e., are both initially caused by and causally sustained by) appropriate connections (either through evolution or through a conditioning process) with instances of the Reward Event.[6]

The theory claims that the ultimate or intrinsic anchors of motivation or desire are Reward Events, that is, that those events are causally primary in the origination and sustaining of specific desires and in the recruiting of external objects—or actions performed on such objects—to be the direct (though not ultimate) objects of motivation or desire.

Two aspects of the structure of the theory are of central concern. The first is that motivational states (including specific desires), cognitive states, and Reward Events are *causally distinct* parts of the theory and play their respective roles through contingent connections with each other, with external states of affairs, and with behavior. The second is that when external objects and/or behaviors performed with respect to those objects are recruited as the direct objects of desire, the focus of desire will indeed be on those external states, but the anchor of the desire (the real causal source of the desire) is and continues to be the Reward Event, and that the connection between focus and anchor is, itself, a contingent connection. These various contingent connections help to determine the contours and explanatory roles of the psychological concepts of motive, desire, and pleasure.

The strategy is this. I first discuss some simpler systems not involving Reward Events and deal briefly with the conceptual issues they raise. I then concentrate on the causal structure of Reward Event Systems and suggest a conceptualization of that structure.

Throughout, I deal only with positive motivation or desire and simply assume, in the spirit of RET, that a roughly parallel story could be told for negative motivation in terms of an internal aversive event or events.

SOME SIMPLER SYSTEMS

System 1: A Reflex System

If a creature, or a subsystem of a creature, is a system of this type, then it is so "wired up" that its detecting a stimulus of a particular type automatically and invariably causes a specific motor response. Failure of the response will be due either to a defect in the sensory detector or to a defect in motor capacity. For example, if the eye and tongue of the toad are so connected, through the toad's brain, that whenever a small, erratically moving object (SEMO) is detected, the tongue zaps the object, then this would be a System I subsystem in the toad. Would motivational concepts have any place in the theory of such a subsystem? Specifically, would hunger play any explanatory role? Such a hypothesized internal state would not play any *differential* explanatory role, accounting for why the toad sometimes zaps SEMOs and sometimes does not when sensory and motor systems are intact, since the toad always zaps under those conditions. In addition, there would be no satiation associated with such hunger. We could, perhaps, say that the toad is always hungry and never gets enough to eat, but this is theoretically unpersuasive. If, as some theorists argue, "motivation refers to the arousal and new direction of specific behaviors and their satiation, and the new arousal and direction of other behaviors, representing shifts in motivations" (Stellar and Stellar 1985, 22), then there would seem to be little conceptual space for hunger as an explanatory concept in this sort of system.

At the same time, if a creature has two such reflex systems, one of which leads to *approach toward* a sensory object and the other of which leads to *withdrawal from* a different sensory object, there is a conceptual temptation to see the creature in quasi-motivational terms. It begins to look like a valenced system, which is differentially responsive to different kinds of stimuli, desiring some and being averse to others. As is often noted, however, this would include an enormous range of both living and nonliving systems. If the individual reflex systems do not sustain motivational concepts, it is not clear why their combination should. Nevertheless, a caution is in order. Natural creatures, and systems within natural creatures, have evolved; we should not expect any clear-cut line, with motivation or desire obviously *not* on one side of the line, and obviously *on* the other side.

System II: A Basic Motivational System

Suppose a creature, with sensory organs and motor capabilities intact, upon detecting food sometimes responds by eating it and sometimes does not eat, and that this difference in response is causally controlled by a variable internal physiological state. Now there seems considerable conceptual space for the motivational concept of hunger. There is also, however, room for much disagreement.

If, for example, someone defines 'hunger' as "the desire to eat," and insists that a desire must have intentional content, and that many creatures who are differentially responsive to food nevertheless lack the cognitive capacities for the appropriate intentional content of the desire to eat, then such a person would deny that any System II involves the motivational state of hunger.

There are other complications. For example, the blowfly "can be aroused to exploratory activity and ingestion upon external stimulation of its taste receptors, but its eating behavior is unaffected by its internal *metabolic* state (Dethier, 1976). Eating is terminated (satiation?) by the development of pressure in the foregut, which stimulates the recurrent nerve" (Stellar and Stellar 1985, 23, my emphasis). Here eating is controlled by a variable internal state (pressure in the foregut), but this is not a metabolic state (which may explain the question mark after the term 'satiation'). In addition, the internal state is not the *initiator* of exploration and ingestion—that seems to be controlled by sensory stimulation—but only its terminator. So if there are good theoretical reasons for tying hunger to a metabolic state, then despite the control and quasi-satiation aspects, one should not say that the blowfly is motivated by hunger.

The blowfly is, of course, a relatively simple system. The conceptual issues become more complex when one considers cybernetic models that have been developed to explain behavior in rats and other more evolved creatures. The systems approach of Toates (1980) is representative.

Toates explains his general method as follows:

> in order to understand the causes of the animal's behaviour we should attempt to model the essential processes in formal terms. . . . by a model we mean a representation which captures the important processes underlying behaviour. . . . Models that take the form of a diagram showing the important processes are much better, and better still is computer simulation. (3-4)

It should also be noted that Toates makes a clear and helpful distinction between levels of explanation. The *functional* level "refers to how behaviour increases the survival and reproductive chances of an animal." For example, "functional explanations tell us how mating increases gene perpetuation chances. . . ." Toates goes on to say, however, that "the functional explanation is of no value in directly explaining the sexual drive of an individual animal. Here our explanation must be in terms of hormone levels, incoming sensory information from a partner, executive brain regions controlling mounting, etc. This is the *causal* analysis. . . ." Toates's models are intended to include factors relevant, not only to the simple environments of the controlled laboratory situation, but also to the animal's natural habitat, and thus the models include everything from physiological states to "decision rules" (4-6).

What is less clear is how Toates sees the implications of his systems approach for specific psychological concepts, such as motivation. On the one hand, he suggests a sort of deconstruction, in which an appeal to motivation is seen as a substitute for more adequate explanations:

> Whether or not a drive concept [The term "drive" appears in a preliminary discussion of the "evolution of the concept of motivation"; no distinction is made between drive and motivation.] is used, or even considered important, depends upon the purpose of the investigation. Where behaviour is being examined, and is clearly dependent upon events within the animal which are poorly understood, then it may prove inescapable to use a word such as drive to indicate the tendency of the animal to perform in a certain way. At other times it may be either misleading, or leading to an intellectual cul-de-sac, to attribute behaviour to a drive, when the only evidence for a drive is the behaviour we are observing. . . . *As more and more evidence about the neural, hormonal, and experiential determinants of behaviour becomes available, it would appear that theoretical drive constructs will suffer natural extinction.* (3, my emphasis)

On the other hand, Toates also suggests a reconstruction of motivational concepts, in which they apply to entire systems, rather than to any distinguishable part of the system. In his general introduction, he says he will "consider the physiological *aspect* of motivation" and will then "consider each motivation system in turn" (6, my emphasis). The relevant chapters in which these systems are discussed have such familiar motivation titles as hunger, thirst, sex, aggression and fear, as well as temperature control and sleep. Here, motivational labels seem to cover all the causal factors influencing a particular kind of behavior.

There is much to recommend an approach that emphasizes the complexity of causes and the importance of ethological and evolutionary information along with more immediate causal factors. But applying motivational labels to whole systems can obscure important distinctions, in much the same way that important distinctions may be obscured when the term 'cognitive' is used to cover all causal factors. RET, by contrast, assigns distinct causal roles to motivation, cognition, and reward. If these psychological concepts continue to be used at all (an issue to be discussed later), this approach is likely to be more theoretically fruitful.

Finally, note that even if one agrees that a System II does have motivational states, there could still be disagreement as to whether the difference in motivational state operates by valencing already noticed stimuli or whether it has a more direct cognitive impact on whether the stimulus is even noticed. There is a need to interpret experiments such as those that have shown that individual neurons in a monkey's brain, which are selectively responsive to the taste and/or the sight of food, respond only when the animal is food-deprived and hungry (Stellar and Stellar 1985, 56).

System III: A Conditioning System

Let us continue with the blowfly. Stellar and Stellar note that, for the blowfly, "food . . . is not a ready reinforcer of new learning" (23). Interestingly, they go on to conclude from this that "the blowfly may have only a rudimentary form of motivated behavior or a precursor of what we see in vertebrates," though they also note that "other invertebrates, like the ant, the bee, and octopus, can learn on the basis of food reward" (24).

Motivation is now being connected to learning, specifically to the ability of a creature to learn through operant conditioning.

Let us say that in a System III, motivation connects with a learning process in which something functions as a reward.[7] In the psychological literature, particularly that officially committed to operational definitions, 'motivation' and 'reward' tend to be closely interdefined through connections with the operant conditioning process. For example, hunger *is* the motivational state that makes food rewarding, and food *is* the reward for the motivational state of hunger. In addition, food is defined as a reward or reinforcer through its role in operant conditioning.[8] There is, however, a tension between the official definitions, in which reward or reinforcement is *defined* in terms of its impact on behavior, and the tendency to view the fact that something is a reward as the *explanation* for this shaping of behavior. When I come to the Reward Event System, I will resolve that tension by separating—causally and definitionally—motivation, behavior, and reward.

Note that in a System III, a motivation such as hunger can be focused on different kinds of food that have different degrees of reward or reinforcement, as measured by operant conditioning. Thus, at this level, there is often a distinction made between degrees of motivation (how hungry is the creature?) and degrees of incentive value (given the same degree of hunger, will the creature learn faster with or work harder for food A or food B?). Now, instead of speaking generically of hunger as the desire for some food or range of foods, one can speak of specific desires for specific kinds of food. Thus, a creature might indeed be hungry, but not hungry enough to desire *that kind* of food.

We should also note that in a System III there is a distinction between a natural, primary, or innate reward, which can operate as a reinforcement in a naive creature that has had no prior experience of the reward, and a secondary or learned reward, which only becomes a reinforcer after the creature has developed a learned association (as in classical conditioning) between it and a primary reward. Once we have secondary or learned rewards, the question can be raised as to their functional autonomy. Do they continue to function as rewards only if periodically reconnected with some primary reward, or can they become functionally autonomous? This is a central issue in the characterization of a Reward Event System.

It might be asked why a System III, which is characterized in terms of the operation of reward or reinforcement, is not itself a Reward Event System. The answer is that it *may* be, but only if there can occur within the creature Reward Events that are causally and functionally distinct from motivation, desire, or operant behavior and thus can be conceptually distinguished from those aspects of the system. Specifically, Reward Events should be able to serve as rewards or reinforcers on their own, independent of any standard primary reward. This should become clearer in our examination of a Reward Event System.

This survey of Systems I, II, and III is not intended to be exhaustive or exclusive. An adequate discussion of the full range of actual biological creatures would need to make many more distinctions and would have to take account of the fact that in more complex creatures there is a hierarchical organization of neurological functions; that with suppression or elimination of the higher levels of organization, simpler systems within the creature take control; and thus, by implication, that higher levels (e.g., sophisticated cognition) can modify the role of lower levels (see Stellar and Stellar 1985, 205-209). I wanted only a sketch of simpler systems to have a contrast with a full-scale Reward Event System. We should keep in mind, however, that even in simpler systems there are possibilities for alternative conceptualizations, under varying degrees of empirical constraint. We should expect this to be even more the case with a Reward Event System.

A REWARD EVENT SYSTEM

Consider a rat who last ate an hour ago. Since then he has been napping and grooming. Now he becomes more active, begins to move about his available home territory (his cage), goes to a bar at one side of the cage, and presses it. This produces three pellets of rat chow, which he eats. He repeats the bar pressing a number of times, each time eating the pellets, and then stops, drinks some water, does a bit of grooming, and takes another nap. Just an average bit of a day in the life of a lab rat.

How would the Reward Event Theory explain what is going on in this sequence of events? First, there is a physiological state within the rat that varies as a function of size of last meal and time since last meal. When this state reaches a critical level, the rat usually becomes restless and looks about for food. (Note that this is not true by definition; it is a standard causal consequence of the physiological state.) We shall say, provisionally, that the rat is in the motivational state of hunger. Second, there are relevant sensory/perceptual events—the rat sees the lever (and sees and smells the pellets). The rat presses the lever because in past operant conditioning when the rat was hungry and pressed the lever, this action was followed by food pellets. In that past conditioning, as well as in the current eating sequence, ingestion of pellets, probably primarily acting through a taste mechanism, sets off a (perhaps dopamine-based) circuit in the brain that is an intrinsic Reward Event. Reward Events function as reinforcement for both the learned bar pressing and the actual eating of the pellets. When enough pellets have been eaten, this causes metabolic/chemical changes that affect the brain, blocking the Reward Events so that eating is no longer rewarding. The rat then ceases to eat.

This is the standard case. I want to bracket, and simply assume as a given, the appropriate perceptual/cognitive states, to concentrate on the motivation and reward aspects. There is the motivational state of hunger, there is the focusing of that hunger on the perceived pellets, there is the eating of the pellets, and there is the Reward Event triggered by that eating. The key claim of the Reward Event Theory is that each of these is a separate, causally and functionally distinct component of the system, that the Reward Event is the central causal key, and that the connections among these components are contingent and can be severed or bypassed. How must the evidence go to sustain this claim, and what are its implications?

First, it must be possible to trigger the Reward Event directly by appropriate stimulation of the brain, bypassing any standard reward such as food. The rat should be able to learn, and be motivated, to produce such brain stimulation.[9]

Second, it should be possible, by blocking the Reward Event (e.g., through the use of chemical dopamine blockers), to sever the standard connection between the physiological state of hunger, perception of food, and eating, so that a creature would be "hungry" but would not eat.[10]

Third, it should be possible to cause eating that is independent of the physiology of hunger and that is causally sustained simply by the triggering of the Reward Event. There would be no satiation in these cases.[11]

Fourth, it should be possible, through appropriate associative conditioning with Reward Events, to cause a creature to ingest otherwise neutral and nonnutritive substances.[12]

What are the conceptual implications of there being such various possible connections and disconnections among components of a Reward Event System?

MOTIVATION: CAUSAL BASE AND FUNCTION

Consider first the internal physiological state tentatively identified as the motivational state hunger. Now note that this state, under the assumptions of RET, *can* exist without causing any tendency to eat.

Furthermore, a creature can be motivated to eat, and to continue to eat, in the absence of this physiological state. Should the state, then, count as hunger, or as any sort of motivational state at all? Shouldn't hunger, as a motivational state, be conceptually linked to moving a creature to eat? Shouldn't hunger be defined *functionally?*

There is appeal in such a position, which is no doubt due at least in part to the fact that the standard case is, overwhelmingly, the usual case. On the other hand, concepts that are to function as part of an explanatory theory should be responsive to new empirical evidence. If the theory is to fit not just standard cases but all cases, we may find that no causal component of the theory supports all the conceptual connections built up from consideration of standard cases.

If we define hunger in purely functional terms, then we will say that a creature that is anorexic and is slowly starving to death is not at all hungry, while a creature that is moved to eat, and to continue eating, a totally nonnutritive substance without ever reaching a condition of satiation, in the functional sense of a state that terminates the feeding, is always hungry. In severing hunger from any standard internal physiological state, we might also be giving up the possibility of grounding the functional state of hunger in a causal state that constitutes a plausible natural kind.

On the other hand, tying hunger to a physiological or metabolic state does allow the rather paradoxical possibility of a creature's being hungry but not at all moved to eat. One could, however, say instead that the physiological state is hunger—is a motivational state—because in the standard case it does, through appropriate connections with Reward Events, function differentially in the causal production and termination of eating.[13]

I don't think there are conclusive arguments for either of these options—which we might call the *purely functional* versus the *causal base* options. Nevertheless, there are reasons to think that the causal base option will prove to be the most fruitful and the most likely to remain responsive to growing research into the intricacies of the causal base of hunger. For instance, a causal base approach could allow the possibility that further research would reveal a quite separate internal causal base, distinct from that of hunger, that can also function in connection with Reward Events as a differential cause of eating and (perhaps) of the termination of eating. There is no a priori necessity (nor would most people think there is) that only hunger can motivate us, or other creatures, to eat.

It should be noted, however, that if the causal base of motivation in general is tied too tightly to physiological or metabolic states, one would be narrowing the concept in a way that would probably exclude a large range of human motivations—moral motivation, the motivation of revenge, and so on. Whether these motives would be excluded would depend on what we might discover down the line about complex motivations, particularly about the relative roles of cognitive and affective states. It might turn out to be theoretically useful to focus on distinctive brain networks, including a large conceptual component, as the differential causal bases that would be the natural kinds for these motivations. Many theorists do speak of the progressive "encephalization" of motivation. The one vital restriction RET would put on brain networks as causal bases of motivation is that these networks *not* include Reward Events. The theory postulates that Reward Events are distinct causes that are necessary to produce and sustain behaviors usually considered the appropriate response to motivational states. The connection between reward and motivation is one of the key contingent connections in the theory.

If causal bases are expanded to include brain networks, then there are further theoretical/conceptual decisions to be made. Should these causal bases be restricted to fairly stable, long-term states, thus (plausibly) putting motivation in the territory of dispositions or habits? If so, then if (again plausibly) desires are understood as having (particularly in humans) a virtually unlimited number of possible intentional objects, so that there would be as many different desires as there are possible objects, and if there is no lower bound on the temporal duration needed for a desire (e.g., a fleeting desire), then there would be a fairly sharp distinction between motivation and desire. This distinction, however, may depend on how the concept of desire is structured by the Reward Event Theory.

DESIRE: ANCHOR AND FOCUS

In our rat, as a Reward Event System, the motivation of hunger has become focused on pellets and on the consummatory action of eating the pellets. With this specificity of focus, there is a natural tendency to speak of desire. The rat desires to eat the pellets. In many theories, either the pellets or the eating of the pellets is the reward that anchors learning. RET says otherwise. It is only when eating the pellets triggers a Reward Event in the brain of the rat that there is the essential causal base for learning and thus for shaping and sustaining specific desires. Nevertheless, in terms of perception and action, the rat is indeed focused on eating pellets. Thus, RET allows for a separation, and merely contingent connection, between the *focus* and the *anchor* of specific desires. And in a creature (such as a human being) with greater conceptual sophistication and reflective awareness, this separation could lead to some rather deep confusions about the ultimate objects of desire.

An ultimate object of desire is often characterized as that which someone desires for its own sake (rather than merely as a means to something else). RET suggests that there is a possible ambiguity in interpreting "for its own sake." Is the interpretation to be in terms of ultimate focus or ultimate anchor? What one suspects is that it is usually taken for granted that these come together at the ultimate level. There have, of course, always been theories of motivation or desire that would separate what a person believes she wants for its own sake from what she really wants, perhaps dividing these between the conscious and unconscious. But if even such natural or primary rewards as food, water, or sex are at most ultimate objects of focus, and are never the ultimate anchors of desire, then the division runs very deep indeed. We then face a conceptual decision—should the ultimate-object label be given to the ultimate focus or the ultimate anchor of desire? There are reasons on both sides.

On the focus side, there is all the behavioral evidence concerning what creatures desire and the introspective evidence concerning what a person desires, what she would report she desires, what she would insist she desires. RET could argue that this is just what one should expect. First, insofar as conditioning works very effectively through only intermittent reinforcement by Reward Events, there would be a constancy of focus not paralleled by a constancy of anchor. In addition, it is very likely that if there are Reward Event Systems, they have evolved to facilitate flexibility of response and the learning of new *outwardly* focused desires that would lead to obtaining those things needed for reproductive success. Nature did not envisage the mainlining of Reward Events. Nevertheless, if we give the object label to the focus of desire, we should keep constantly in mind (or so RET says) that these objects do *not* provide the *fundamental causal* explanation for sustaining desire and thus for the actions of the creature.

Why not, then, give the object label to the anchor of motivation and desire—the Reward Events? Doing so would provide a theoretical neatness in bringing together focus and anchor and would provide a deep monism of the ultimate objects of desire. It would also connect with, and perhaps help explain, the perennial appeal of hedonism (though more on that when we examine the concepts of reward and pleasure). Granted, this alternative would seem more paradoxical to many, but any separation of focus and anchor is bound to generate paradoxes with respect to concepts that assumed their congruence. On the other hand, a monistic interpretation of the ultimate objects of desire would lose touch with both the wide variety and the specificity of desires. It would also tend to obscure evolutionary function, which depends on external focus. Finally, it would present something of a dilemma with respect to the relations among the concepts of motivation, desire, and reward. If one wishes to keep the concept of motivation closely tied to a natural kind causal base distinct from reward, and which at least for primary or innate rewards is closely tied to physiological needs, then one must come to terms with the fact that there seems to be no physiological need for, and thus no independent motivational state to causally connect with, Reward Events (or at least ESB generated Reward Events).[14] In a way, this lack of a physiological need for Reward Events themselves is to be expected, if Reward Event Systems evolved as facilitators for primary rewards that do connect with motivational states. If, however, one now speaks of Reward Events as the ultimate objects of desire, desire is even further disconnected from motivation, as well as from variety and external focus.

REWARD AND PLEASURE

Before we examine the key causal piece of the Reward Event Theory and the conceptual issues it generates, it may help to review the overall causal structure of the theory and the labels we have, provisionally, put on some of those pieces. First, there are variable internal states, often (though not necessarily) physiological or metabolic, that *in standard cases* are the differential causes for some important class of behavior, such as eating. We have given these states the motivation label (e.g., hunger). Second, there are a large number of internal states that play a role similar to motivational states but have a greater specificity of focus and may or may not be related to some standard motivational state. We have given these the desire label. Third, there are the many different external objects or states of affairs that are the focus of most desires. Fourth, there are the appropriate actions performed with respect to these external objects, which in some cases may be considered consummatory actions. We have noted that we could call some of these external objects the ultimate objects of desire, but only if it is recognized that they do *not* provide the ultimate causal explanation for the focusing of desire, the sustaining of desire, and the production of actions with respect to such objects. That role is played by our final causal piece—the Reward Events. Motivation (or desire), external objects, and behavior become causally connected only if there are appropriate contingent causal connections with Reward Events.

What would be an appropriate label for events that play this contingent causal role? I will continue to use the label Reward Events, but with the warning that this label carries a lot of baggage from all the psychological theories that define reward operationally or behavioristically. Reward, in such theories is simply a label for the fact that an object or event shapes behavior or reinforces learning, rather than an explanation for that fact. In addition, the reward is often identified as an external object (food) or the consummatory behavior performed on that object (eating the food). But in RET, the key events are internal brain events that *explain* the focusing of desire and the consummatory behavior.

How, then, should we interpret Reward Events? Let us note another tradition in the literature dealing with these brain events, particularly that dealing with electrical stimulation of the brain (ESB). The tradition speaks of pleasure events in the brain and particularly notes that in brain-stimulation experiments with humans, the subjects do report that the experience is pleasurable. Granting that such introspective reports are not available from other creatures, might there be good theoretical reasons for interpreting Reward Events as pleasure events?

Remember that in RET, an external object or state of affairs is an object of desire, and serves to shape behavior, if and only if it is contingently connected with internal Reward Events. As we saw, this contingency of connection allows the conceptual separation and empirical uncoupling of the focus and anchor of desire. One of the theoretical benefits of such uncoupling is that it allows for an explanation—a causal explanation—for why external objects are the objects of desire. There is also a conceptual price, however. In this view, there is no longer anything intrinsic to such objects that can either explain or rationalize their being objects of desire. And if a creature is consciously focused on an external object or state of affairs as a goal, and if that creature supposes that it is clear, from the nature of that goal, why it is her ultimate goal, then she is radically mistaken. There is, in other words, an opacity to the standard objects of desire or motivation, in the sense that they do not and could not provide any insight into why they are goals.[15]

What, now, of the Reward Events themselves? To simplify, let us focus on cases, such as ESB, where a single event is both the anchor and the focus of desire. In ESB cases, it is not possible to uncouple anchor and focus; a Reward Event cannot be uncoupled from itself. Now, if we ask why the Reward Event is rewarding, is such a compelling object of desire, we can no longer give the causal answer of linking it contingently to some further event. It would, then, be natural to assume that there must be something about the event itself that explains why it is rewarding.

We can now understand some of the motivation for interpreting Reward Events as pleasure events. There has been, of course, much debate about the concept of pleasure. Theories have ranged from its being a specific sensation, to its being a phenomenal aspect of experience, to its being an hedonic tone of experience, to its being simply a positive attitude toward something (as being "pleased with X"), or a disposition to pursue X. One central tradition, cutting across some of these distinctions, has seen in pleasure a kind of experience that can function both to provide a causal explanation of desire and to provide a rational insight into why it is an object of desire. (Think of Bentham's use of pleasure as the anchor for both motivation and evaluation.) We could escape any ultimate opacity of desire, since it would seem to be rationally self-evident why creatures desire—are motivated to obtain—pleasure. This double role for pleasure—as both explanation of and rationalization for desire—may explain some of the perennial appeal of traditional hedonism.

So, is RET a form of hedonism? It is, but only if we make this important qualification—Reward Events, as the final causal piece in the theory, cannot play the double role required by the central tradition of hedonism. Nothing can play that role, and so desire and motivation are opaque all the way down.

The dilemma is this. If Reward Events are to provide rational insight into ultimate desire or motivation, then there must be something in their intrinsic qualities that provides insight into why they are the objects of desire. But Reward Events function in the Reward Event Theory to provide a causal explanation of desire. It is a contingent fact that Reward Events do cause and sustain desire and do shape behavior. One might suppose one could resolve this dilemma by providing a functional definition of pleasure in terms of this causal role. This would conceptually connect pleasure with desire, but at a price. First, there would be serious objections from nonhedonists, who would argue that the mere fact that something functions as an ultimate cause of desire is not sufficient reason to call that something pleasure (though this would probably reflect a suspicion that the concept is still carrying a lot of traditional baggage). Second, interpreting Reward Events as pleasure events in this purely functional sense would mean that their being pleasure events is no longer a further explanation for why such events cause desire; it would simply be a labeling of that fact. We are faced, once again, with a choice between an intrinsic quality, causal-base interpretation of a concept and a purely functional interpretation. Neither choice is going to give us both causal explanation and rational insight.

Is there, then, any reason to interpret Reward Events as pleasure events? There are the introspective reports of human subjects of ESB, and while these subjects may be using unreconstructed concepts, there seems no reason to discount totally what they say. In addition, interpreting Reward Events as pleasure events captures something significant about the causal structure of RET, namely, that Reward Events are independent causes of desire and of the shaping of behavior; this, in turn, provides some of the theoretical motivation for interpreting pleasure in terms of intrinsic qualities, an interpretation for which I will argue. Interpreting reward operationally or behavioristically can obscure this independent causal role. Finally, the deep monism of RET, which anchors all positive motivation and desire in a single basic kind of event, does parallel the deep monism of traditional hedonistic theories of motivation. In sum, the structure of RET emphasizes that in addition to cognitive states (beliefs, etc.) and motivational states (desires, etc.), there is a further independent type of cause needed for the explanation of behavior. Interpreting these causal events as pleasure events is making the theoretical commitment that *affective* states play a distinct and essential causal role.

Is it, however, persuasive to think of pleasure as merely contingently connected with desire or motivation? Could it make sense to think of a creature experiencing pleasure events but not being at all motivated to pursue them?

Such a conceptual move is bound to provoke resistance not only from practicing scientists committed to operationalizing all concepts but also from philosophers. For example, Findlay (1961) has argued:

> were pleasure and unpleasure peculiar *qualities* [presumably intrinsic qualities] of experience, as loud and sweet are peculiar qualities of what comes before us in sense-experience, it would be a gross, empirical accident that we uniformly sought the one and avoided the other, as it is a gross empirical accident in the case of the loud or the sweet, and this is of all suppositions the most incredible and absurd. Plainly it is in some sense almost trivially necessary that we should want pleasure (or *not* want unpleasure). . . . (177)

We should also note, however, that Findlay goes on to say, "But there is another sense in which there is an *a priori* connection between wants and pleasure which is remote from the tautological, the sense in which the vivid, believing thought of something as likely to please *almost* inevitably generates a want for it, a want which is a *consequence* rather than a presupposition of its being thought pleasant" (178, my emphasis). This seems to be discussing a fairly uniform, though not inevitable, causal connection between pleasure (or more precisely, the thought of pleasure) and a want, a connection more reasonably seen as contingent, not a priori.

There has been an interesting suggestion by Katz (1982) that seeing pleasure and motivation as only contingently connected may be the best way to conceptualize certain empirical phenomena:

> If we are not, then, to class all environmentally sensitive animal movements as motivated, where are we to draw the line? Wise apparently views hedonic arousal as necessarily involved. So we might allow behavior to be called "motivated" just when past or present hedonic (or, more broadly, affective) arousal figures essentially in its etiology. Given what we

know of the physiology involved, we should stand a fair chance of thus picking out at once a functional kind and a physiological kind as well— perhaps involving central dopamine systems, among others. But is affect a sufficient (and, as we are assuming, necessary) condition for motivation? While there exists a use among some psychologists that includes emotion, drive, and even some homeostatic self-regulation, this seems rather broad for the core meaning. The 'smile' response elicited by sucrose and the 'disgust' response by quinine, when placed in the mouth of the midbrain rat (Grill & Norgren 1978a;b)—and similar phenomena in the apparently comparable anencephalic human infant (Steiner 1973, as cited in Grill & Norgren 1978a)—may be hedonic responses of creatures incapable of acquired motivation or appetitive behavior of any kind. If motivation—like desire—requires the ability to maintain an acquired central image of a goal, affect (and dopamine or whatever) may not be enough. (60)

This passage clearly interprets hedonic events (i.e., pleasure events) as having only contingent connections with motivation and desire, which connections may be lacking, as in the midbrain and anencephalic cases. It is equally clear that whether the connections are contingent depends on how one conceptualizes motivation. Thus, whether it makes sense for a creature to experience pleasure events without those events becoming the object of any motivation or desire is an issue at the interface of the conceptual and the empirical. Once these different conceptualizations are recognized, we can no longer just assume, a priori, that pleasure is necessarily the object of desire. This undercuts the possibility of there being a rational insight into why pleasure motivates or is desired. To the degree that traditional hedonism assumed such necessary connections and/or rational insight, we must say that even if we interpret Reward Events as pleasure events, the Reward Event Theory is hedonistic only in a revisionist sense.

There is another very important respect in which the "hedonized" version of RET is not traditional hedonism. The latter, as both a psychological and value theory, has tended to assume a certain metric of pleasure, with motivation or desire tied to that metric. It may be assumed, for example, that the dimensions of pleasure are degrees of intensity and duration, and that degrees of motivation will obviously be a function of just those two dimensions. For RET, on the other hand, the metric of pleasure events may be a matter of intensity and duration (as is suggested by ESB experiments), but the relationship to strength and/or duration of motivation or desire must be established by empirical evidence. Which schedules of reinforcement by Reward Events are in fact most effective? And by which measures of effectiveness? The evidence is complex and gives little support to a simple "more is better or stronger" assumption (see Stellar and Stellar 1985; Wise 1982).

BRAIN REWARD AND BEHAVIOR: NEUROPSYCHOLOGY AND RET

RET aims to be responsive to ongoing developments in neuropsychology. Since the classic experiments by Olds and Milner in the 1950s, the scientific literature on brain-reward systems has expanded exponentially. Some of the key issues raised are as follows:

1. Are there distinct locations in the brain at which electrical stimulation will produce the reward effects? (The answer is clearly yes.)
2. Do these distinct locations nevertheless activate some common pathways, so that it is theoretically plausible to speak of a single reward system? (The evidence is mixed, and no strong consensus exists; RET postulates a unity of Reward Events.)
3. Do the common pathways (assuming there are such) depend on a specific neurotransmitter, such as dopamine? (Mixed evidence, with dopamine-based systems remaining the most plausible candidate.)
4. Does ESB activate natural reward centers that operate in the rewarding effects of all natural, innate rewards, such as food, water, and sex? (This is assumed by many experimenters, but evidence is still sufficiently inconclusive to allow much debate. This is a key assumption of RET.)
5. Are all learned motivations functionally dependent on the operation of reward events? (Thoroughly speculative at present, with the evidence as complex and inconclusive as debates over learning theory and motivation, particularly human motivation; this is probably RET's most vulnerable assumption.)

Rather than attempt the impossible task of reviewing all the literature, I will concentrate on some of the work of Roy Wise. I will emphasize certain conceptual/theoretical issues raised by Wise's methodological statements. Specifically, I will defend RET's conception of intrinsic reward and contrast it with Wise's more operationalized conceptions of reward, as part of a more general discussion of the constraints on adequacy of explanation.

Wise's "anhedonia hypothesis" (1982) is offered as an explanation for the impact of neuroleptics on operant behavior. His focus in this paper could be seen as quite narrow and primarily concerned with the role of dopamine in reward, but a number of Wise's statements make broader claims about a general theory of motivation. In addition, his statements in this particular paper are closest in spirit to RET, at least under one possible interpretation, and raise quite clearly the issue of pleasure as an explanatory concept.

Neuroleptics are dopamine-blockers, and when administered to test creatures, they cause various disruptions in "the learning and performance of operant habits motivated by a variety of positive reinforcers, including food, water, brain stimulation, intravenous opiates, stimulants, and barbiturates. . . . Neuroleptics also blunt the euphoric impact of amphetamine in humans" (39). There is also evidence that under the impact of neuroleptics, "a normally effective reinforcer fails to establish adequately *learned associations* in classical conditioning paradigms when no (or minimal) response demands are made on the animal" (41, my emphasis).

The anhedonia hypothesis concerning this range of phenomena is that "neuroleptics blunt the hedonic impact of rewards (reinforcers that presumably have positive hedonic impact). . . ." In addition, since the hedonic impact is associated with (identified with?) certain dopamine-based brain events, the hypothesis suggests "a role for brain dopamine in the *mediation* of motivational phenomena of reward and reinforcement" (39).

The above quotations from Wise offer the blunting or blocking of hedonic impact as the explanation for why neuroleptics disrupt the ability of externally identified rewards to generate and sustain learning and performance. This explanation seems to entail that in the standard cases, it is the hedonic impact of the rewards that explains their effectiveness. In other words, it is the fact that experiences of pleasure are produced that explains why, for example, eating food is (usually) rewarding.

In most of the experiments cited by Wise the subjects were rats, but he also refers to evidence from experiments with human subjects, as in the following passage:

Finally, human reports indicate that neuroleptics blunt the reinforcing effects of intravenous amphetamine. Here the measure is the subjective euphoric effect of a given dose of amphetamine, rated in standardized conditions including placebo and other pharmacological treatments. While amphetamine euphoria has been rated as normal or enhanced under other treatments, it is rated as reduced by neuroleptic treatment (Gunne, Änggard & Jönsson 1972; Jönsson, Änggard & Gunne 1971). Thus it appears that it is not only the reinforcing impact but also the hedonic impact of amphetamine which is blunted by neuroleptic treatment. (47)

One could read the final sentence in this quotation as making a distinction between reinforcing impact (behavioral effects) and hedonic impact (pleasure event), with the latter as the contingent cause of the former. This would be the interpretation most consistent with RET. It is complicated, however, by Wise's counting the rating of the "subjective euphoric effect" (the pleasure) as the "measure" of reinforcing effect, as if the degree of euphoria were itself the reinforcement impact or as if one could simply assume a simple linear correlation between degree of euphoria and degree of reinforcement. Nevertheless, Wise does seem to be giving a central explanatory role to a nonbehavioral conception of pleasure, as indicated when he says, "The critical test of the anhedonia hypothesis would be in man, of course, since in the rat inferences about subjective hedonic impact can at best be only tentative" (50).

When Wise later develops a theory of addiction (Wise and Bozarth 1987), however, he backs away from any hedonic explanation, on the basis both of some directly contrary evidence and of methodological qualms concerning the role of nonoperationalized concepts in theories.

Wise and Bozarth criticize dependence theories of addiction, in which addiction is identified in terms of compulsive drug seeking and dependence is defined as a distress syndrome that develops when habitual drug intake is discontinued or pharmacologically blocked. They note that "the notion of physical dependence offers a potential explanation of addiction that meets the first criterion for a heuristic theory; it is not merely renaming the phenomenon it attempts to explain (470).

The second criterion, however, is that a theory identify "a common denominator for such diverse conditions as cocaine addiction, alcohol addiction, and heroin addiction. . . . The assumption is that a common denominator will have *heuristic* value, and that our learning about one addiction will facilitate our learning about another" (469). And it is claimed that the available evidence is "inconsistent with the view that physical dependence is either a necessary or a sufficient condition for addiction" (470; the evidence is summarized on 470-473).

These methodological statements are quite consistent with RET, which also insists that defining reward operationally is inconsistent with using reward as an explanation for the shaping of behavior. RET defines reward in terms of intrinsic positive affect, and then asserts that these Reward Events cause the focusing of desire and the shaping of behavior.

The methodological statements are also consistent with Wise's own anhedonia hypothesis, so we might at this point expect Wise and Bozarth to develop a "hedonia" theory of addiction. And, indeed, they do say that "the only existing positive reinforcement view of addiction that might qualify as an explanatory theory identifies positive reinforcement with drug euphoria. In this view drugs are addicting (establish compulsive habits) because they produce euphoria or positive affect. . . ." (474).

Wise and Bozarth go on, however, to offer two criticisms of euphoria theories. First, they claim that human beings are more likely to report that initial interactions with opiates, ethanol, and nicotine are dysphoric rather than euphoric. This claim would pose a serious problem for RET, if the literature on addiction supported the view that these drug experiences are consistently dysphoric. The evidence seems otherwise, however; one researcher even boldly asserts, "For anyone with a biological education it is clear that the development of dependence is based on pleasurable experiences via the brain reward systems. I do not know of any case where an individual has developed a dependence upon drugs that give unpleasant sensations" (Bejerot 1987, 177). Bejerot no doubt overstates his case, and the disagreement between Bejerot and Wise and Bozarth may depend on the significance attached to *initial* interactions with drugs, but the consensus among researchers is that addictive-drug experiences are on the whole pleasant.

Wise and Bozarth's second criticism of euphoria theories is methodological and indicates Wise's second thoughts about any appeal to nonoperationalized concepts (as in his own anhedonia hypothesis). The problem, they argue, is that "euphoria is a condition that cannot be observed but must rather be inferred in lower animals. . . . We have no *independent* criteria for euphoria in lower animals above and beyond the evidence that the animals will self-administer the drug or that the drug will increase the self-administration of brain stimulation reward" (474).

RET does make an explicit commitment to a nonoperational definition of reward, and this definition requires both appeal to introspective reports by humans and speculative extrapolation to "lower animals." By contrast, Wise and Bozarth claim that "what is needed is a theory of reinforcement that predicts the reinforcing effects of drugs on the basis of some independent set of observations that can be quantified and compared between humans and lower animals" (474). The Wise and Bozarth theory claims that reinforcement (defined operationally, which makes it definitionally equivalent to addictive behavior) is homologous with psychomotor stimulation (approach behaviors) and that these two phenomena derive from a common biological (neurological) mechanism—"the forebrain dopamine systems and one or more of their efferent connections" (481).

What can I say to this methodological challenge to RET? First, if one's criterion for adequacy of theory is simply that one have a reliable, independent predictor of the addictive potential of various substances (a very understandable goal given the practical urgency of problems of addiction), then one can acknowledge that the Wise and Bozarth theory, if correct, would meet this test of adequacy. But many of the above methodological statements suggest rather stronger criteria of adequacy.

Specifically, one wants a theory to explain why certain substances are addictive. Would the Wise and Bozarth theory do this? If one equates explanation with reliable prediction, perhaps so. But is such prediction adequate for explanation? If two phenomena, A and B, have a common cause, C, then A may be a reliable predictor of B, and vice-versa, but it seems more plausible to say that C explains the occurrence of both A and B, rather than saying either that A explains B or that B explains A. This appeal to a common cause seems to be the form of the Wise and Bozarth theory. A postulated common cause, C (certain neurological events, tentatively identified with "forebrain dopamine systems and one or more of their efferent connections"), is stated to be the common cause of both A (reinforcement, defined as the operant behavior that is the addictive behavior) and B (approach behaviors). This interpretation of their theory is tentative, since there are few explicit statements about what causes what. (In addition, one begins to wonder if there is such a clear distinction between the relevant operant behavior, which must involve some approach, and the presumably independent approach behavior.) There is no suggestion that the approach behaviors (B) cause the reinforcement (A). Thus B, while it may be a good indicator of A, does not in any stricter sense explain A. It is C that explains both A and B, and C is not defined operationally, but is rather identified with certain neurological events. How does this compare with RET?

First, a point about explanation at the functional level identified by Toates—that is, at the level of ethology and evolution. It would make a good deal of biological sense if neurological mechanisms had evolved in such a way that activities promoting biological fitness trigger Reward Events (nutritious food tastes good) that then cause approach behavior. Seek the pleasant, which is a reasonably reliable sign of the beneficial (though not infallible, as demonstrated by the eager ingestion of saccharine).

Wise and Bozarth could run a parallel explanation, substituting a neurological description for a description in terms of positive affect. A move to neurological explanations raises fundamental methodological issues. Will the best explanations of the future be framed entirely in neurological terms, eliminating all use of psychological concepts, be they motivation, reward, or whatever? This may be the direction in which Wise and Bozarth are heading, but as long as explanation is still intended to be psychological, I would suggest that despite its presumed methodological difficulties, RET gives a more plausible explanation of addiction than does the Wise and Bozarth theory.

Despite this advantage in terms of psychological theory, RET is committed to the view that specific brain events are involved in pleasure and pain, and this commitment raises difficult issues in the philosophy of mind. Are pleasure events identical with specific brain events? Is the positive affect of such events merely epiphenomenal to their neurology? Which descriptions of the events—the psychological affect descriptions or the neurological descriptions—will provide the best explanations for their effects on behavior?

I do not attempt to resolve these issues. Instead, I make the following hypothetical claim. *If* psychological explanations remain scientifically useful (and perhaps indispensable), and are not to be eliminated in favor of purely neurological explanations, then there are good reasons for including, among the relevant aspects of psychological states, not only intentional content, but also positive (or negative) hedonic tone, which does not have such content. RET is a challenge to the adequacy of any psychological theory that would explain how we work solely in terms of informational or content-driven states, whether those be beliefs, desires, intentions, or a more sophisticated revision of these folk psychological concepts.

EGOISM AND THE BY-PRODUCT THEORY REVISITED

Let us return briefly to our opening discussion of psychological egoism and to the issues raised by the By-Product Theory of Motivation.

Internalism Versus Externalism of the Ultimate Objects of Motivation

One of the least plausible aspects of psychological egoism was its insistence that the only ultimate objects of motivation, *what* we want for its own sake, are certain of our own psychological states. To a degree, we have dealt with this issue by distinguishing between the focus of motivation and the anchor of motivation, but the challenge is still there and could be phrased as follows: Even if something like RET is true, why doesn't that merely tell us more about the mechanism of motivation, about *why* we have the many different objects of motivation we do have? Why should that mechanism itself count as the only ultimate object? Several comments are in order.

First, we should remember the peculiar dominance of the ESB experience in rats and of some drug experiences in humans. It is as if these experiences, these Reward Events, cut loose from any distracting association with external objects or events, were for the first time revealed in their full motivational strength. Thus, the operation of the Reward Event in more mixed phenomena may be buffered in such a way that focus shifts, but the Reward Event would still be the aspect of these more complex experiences that we are motivated to obtain.

Second, there are good evolutionary reasons why our focus should be outward. A creature could neither survive nor evolve if it had a dominant preference for an internal psychological state that it could somehow produce directly, instead of through obtaining food, water, sex, and so on. The ability to mainline Reward Events is something of an artifact, which may also explain why creatures have not evolved defenses against its dominance when it is available.

Third, there are advantages to having motivation depend upon Reward Events that are only contingently connected with external events and objects; such contingent dependence could well be the motivational key to flexibility of response and to the learning of new goals.

Fourth, the contingency of connection between the ultimate goal of the Reward Event and sundry external objects is also suggested by several other human phenomena. One of the most familiar is what could be called the Wordsworth Effect—the loss of the sense of intrinsic delight in scenes and activities that formerly were strongly motivating, say the natural landscapes of childhood. At a greater extreme, there are the cases of extreme depression, often part of the manic-depressive or bipolar syndrome. Often, people afflicted with this disorder report that while in the depression phase, they cannot even get out of bed to perform vital functions, such as feeding their own children. Might a massive failure of connections with Reward Events account for this massive failure of motivation? A prominent symptom of depression is not only failure of motivation but also anhedonia, a pervasive loss of the ability to experience pleasure. If anhedonia is not merely one more symptom but the key to loss of motivation, we are close to RET.

Consider, finally, the challenge of cases where a person seems to pursue a goal that can only come to fruition after she is dead. The person never will experience that fruition, nor, a fortiori, any (possible) associated Reward Event. So how can Reward Events be sustaining such motivation?

Any adequate theory of human motivation must of course take account of the enormous role played by our cognitive capacities. We should expect to find, in that charming phrase from the technical literature, the "encephalization of motivation." So, with respect to these problem cases, the story might go several ways. With respect to novel, future goals whose fruition one could expect to experience, one might well have beliefs, grounded in analogy with already experienced goals, concerning the possibility of appropriate Reward Events. One would *expect* to be satisfied. However, not only is this in many cases at least introspectively implausible, but it is also antithetical to the real spirit of RET. For on this hypothesis, a *belief* (granted, a belief about some future Reward Event) would be intrinsically motivating. Furthermore, this hypothesis would not handle cases where one does not expect to experience the fruition of the goal.

Far more likely is the hypothesis that we have the ability to envisage future, or possible, or merely imaginary states of affairs, and that such envisagement, particularly when vivid, can link directly to the Reward Event. (Isn't that what fantasy is about?) Any associated motivation would be cycled through and dependent upon the Reward Event. Clearly, this linkage is an empirical issue. One of the great advantages of finding a neurological basis of the Reward Event is that doing so could provide a way of gathering fairly strong evidence. It would be difficult to determine introspectively whether one was being motivated solely by a present belief about a future state of affairs, or whether a present satisfaction arising from the envisaging of that state of affairs was the real motivational key, but if we could test neurologically for the presence or absence of the Reward Event, this would be important independent evidence.

It is possible to interpret some of the brain-damage cases discussed by Damasio (1994) as providing relevant evidence. Many of the patients observed by Damasio and others "were unable to organize future activity" and were also "less able than others to experience pleasure and react to pain" (58). Damasio interprets the cases in terms of his own distinctive theory of the nature and role of emotions and feelings (see my discussion in chapter 1). He argues that in normal individuals (by implication it is what is lacking in these patients), "When the bad outcome connected with a given response option comes into mind, however fleetingly, you experience an unpleasant gut feeling [assuming appropriate prior associative learning about the outcome]" (173); correspondingly, the thought of favorable outcomes triggers pleasant gut feelings. Since Damasio interprets feelings as perceptions of bodily states, he calls these gut feelings "somatic markers." He applies his theory to the issue of motivation directed to the future:

> This general account also applies to the choice of actions whose immediate consequences are negative, but which generate positive future outcomes. An example is the enduring of sacrifices *now* in order to obtain benefits later. . . . The immediate prospect is unpleasant but the thought of a future advantage creates a positive somatic marker and that overrides the tendency to decide against the immediately painful option. This positive somatic marker which is triggered by the image of a good future outcome must be the base for the enduring of unpleasantness as a preface to potentially better things. (175)

RET interprets Damasio's positive (or negative) somatic markers as Reward Events (or aversion events) and argues that the motivational role is played by positive or negative hedonic tone rather than by any intentional content, even that directed to our own bodies. RET also emphasizes that a present Reward Event can be associated with the thought of a future state of affairs that the person having the thought will not experience. RET and Damasio's theory do agree, however, that the mere thought of, or information about, some possible outcome, in the absence of appropriate feelings, cannot motivate action.

A final comment on sustaining motivation, as displayed in the long-term pursuit of goals: A full theory would need an adequate account of the nature and role of habit and whether it can operate in full autonomy from any Reward Events. We should remember, however, that creatures condition very effectively with intermittent rewards rather than rewards on every trial; indeed, intermittent and unpredictable schedules of reinforcement produce the response patterns that are most resistant to extinction.

Monism Versus Pluralism of the Ultimate Objects of Motivation

How many ultimate objects of motivation are there? I have been sketching a monistic answer to that question—only one, the Reward Event. However, since RET is intended as the sketch of an empirical theory, we should be flexible here. What even counts as one kind of event or object is highly relative to theory and interest. In the literature on ESB in the rat, there is both the emphasis on the phenomenon as a potentially unifying paradigm across other currently recognized forms of motivation and also a constant experimental search for different ESB locations that would be differentially associated with hunger, or thirst, or what have you.

In addition, it must be admitted that as the term 'motivation' is currently used in the psychological literature, it is seen as a pluralistic phenomenon. More accurately, there is a certain flexibility, perhaps even ambiguity, in what is being focused on.

One might, for different purposes, wish to emphasize the differences among the physiological states (so there would be many different motives) or the differences among the external behaviors and objects (so there would be many different objects of motivation). But if physiological states become motives and if behaviors or objects become objects of motivation if and only if they become connected in the appropriate way with the Reward Event, then this is a kind of deep monism, which could be expressed by saying that there is only one basic motive and only one basic object of motivation.

We might note the implications this kind of monism would have for the egoism issue. In one sense, one would still be able to make all the distinctions the anti-egoist wishes to make. Let us say that according to RET, only the Reward Event is ultimately or intrinsically rewarding or motivating. However, many other behaviors, events, thoughts, or what have you would, either through a learning process or by being "wired in" that way, connect directly to the Reward Event. Let us say that when so connected (and this could change), they are then directly rewarding or motivating. (The contrast would be with those behaviors one would be motivated to perform only because they are seen as means to that which is directly rewarding.)[16] Now note that there could be two different individuals, one of whom finds the suffering of others directly rewarding and the other of whom finds helping others directly rewarding. Deep down, they share Reward Event motivation, but for social and moral purposes it is the differences that count. They are very different kinds of people, and of course that matters. But if the anti-egoist wants to claim that some people are ultimately or intrinsically motivated by, for example, perception of the needs of others, then if RET is correct, they are wrong about that.

Direction of Causation

Is desire or satisfaction causally primary? Do we desire X because we have found it satisfying, or do we find it satisfying because we already desire it?

At the level of our commonsense psychology, the phenomena seem a very mixed bag. Sometimes we experience something for the first time, find it enormously satisfying, and thereafter desire it. Sometimes we desire something, pursue it, and on obtaining it, don't find it satisfying. And sometimes we seem to find the obtaining of a goal satisfying precisely because we have wanted it so long and worked so hard for it.

Let us focus on just one fairly basic case—the desire for food and the satisfaction of eating—and use it to outline the deep empirical structure of RET. This is an appropriate case precisely because the scientific literature on which I have been drawing seems to answer the direction-of-causation question in the opposite way from RET. As already noted, hunger is often defined as the internal condition that makes food rewarding, and that definition does seem to give desire the causal priority. Some of this impression may be an artifact of the official, operational definitions, but the issues are, or can be, empirical.

Suppose that the Reward Event is identified neurologically. Also suppose that there is an independent, physiological identification of hunger, the internal condition that usually motivates a creature to eat and seems to make the eating rewarding. Now suppose that the neurological event and the physiological state can be independently controlled so as to produce the following experimental situations.

First, we determine that the creature is in the physiological state of hunger. We allow him to eat, but we suppress the neurological Reward Event. Suppose that the result is that the creature soon ceases trying to eat—seems no longer motivated to eat—even though the hunger condition continues or intensifies. (Have we modeled anorexia?)

In the second experiment, we determine that the creature is in a condition of satiety and thus would not ordinarily be motivated to eat. Now we artificially induce ingestion of food and at the same time trigger the Reward Event. Suppose that the result of this experiment is that the creature now begins to eat and continues to eat as long as the Reward Event is triggered. (Clearly, we are artificially bracketing any aversive events resulting from such overeating.)

Such Mill's Methods results would certainly suggest that the Reward Event—the satisfaction event—is causally primary. When the Reward Event is absent, there is no motivation (here, in the sense of actually being moved to eat); when it is present, there is. On the other hand, it might not work out that way. It might turn out that in the absence of the Reward Event (case one), the creature is still moved to eat, and that in its presence (case two), it is not.

Consider those two conflicting results for our experiments and their implications for the By-Product Theory and for RET.

The By-Product Theory is consistent with the second set of results of our experiments. On this theory, creatures are intrinsically motivated to pursue a number of different kinds of objects or to perform a number of different kinds of actions with respect to those objects. In many instances, though not all, when the object of motivation is obtained, this causes a Reward Event, but the occurrence of such events plays no, or at least no central, role in producing or sustaining motivation. Such Reward Events are mere by-products of the essential machinery that explains the creature's actions.

RET predicts the first set of results. On this theory, the Reward Event mechanism has evolved to play a central, functional role in the behavior of many organisms. Either through the evolutionary history of the organism or through its individual learning history, the Reward Event will have developed contingent connections with other physiological states, with perceived external events, with sundry cognitive states, and with various tendencies to action, in such a way that the Reward Event is the central causal key, an affective key, to why creatures do what they do when and where they do it.

SUMMARY

This, then, is the Reward Event Theory's answer to why we do what we do. At the center of the theory are Reward Events, which are both intrinsically positive and intrinsically motivating. That such events are intrinsically motivating is the central empirical claim of RET, and I have offered in support of the claim a variety of empirical evidence from neuropsychology. That such events are intrinsically positive is also, I believe, an empirical claim in the sense that it provides an accurate description of an important intrinsic quality of experience. This is, however, a highly contested description, and in that sense, the claim is as much conceptual/theoretical as empirical; correspondingly, arguments for this claim must appeal, not only to the direct evidence of our experience, but also to the theoretical advantages of conceptualizing Reward Events in terms of an intrinsic, positive quality that does not, as such, have any intentional content. I have already given some of those arguments, but I will return regularly to this issue, since both in psychological theory and in value theory there are influential, competing conceptualizations of pleasure (and of pain) as relational properties of different sorts.

It should be clear by now that RET, as a theory of motivation, is a form of psychological hedonism. One of the theoretical advantages of my conceptualization of pleasure is that it makes what I will call narrow psychological hedonism a clearly empirical theory. In the next chapter I will make this case and will spell out more explicitly the postulated role of Reward Events in both classical and operant conditioning, thus bringing the theory into contact with much standard psychological learning theory and thereby expanding its empirical base beyond the neuropsychological evidence I have emphasized in this chapter.

3

PSYCHOLOGICAL HEDONISM AS AN EMPIRICAL THEORY

The Reward Event Theory, as a psychological theory, is subject to empirical constraints at several levels, corresponding to different levels or types of explanation. These have been mentioned at various points in the previous chapter, but it may help to review them more systematically; doing so should clarify, reemphasize, and defend one of the key conceptual moves of RET—that Reward Events are intrinsically positive and have only contingent connections with other aspects of our psychology, including any sorts of responses, desires, motivations, and even cognitions. This contingency of connection is bound to seem puzzling, particularly if one considers the possibility of all such connections being severed and perhaps even replaced by quite opposite connections. What could it possibly mean, it might be asked, for Reward Events to be *positive* if, for example, the creature experiencing them were motivated to avoid them, expressed negative attitudes toward them, desired that the experience be terminated, and even reported (expressed the belief) that the experience was awful?[1]

I shall work toward these questions first by considering some *nonempirical* forms of psychological hedonism and then by sketching some possible psychologies that may seem strange but are not, I think, a priori impossible.

First, I do not believe that any form of psychological hedonism should make it a *conceptual* truth that all ultimate motivation is directed toward or caused by pleasure. Many have wanted to maintain that at least sometimes we are motivated by the thought that our action will bring about an external state of affairs (such as, perhaps, the well-being of another individual) or that we are motivated by that thought plus an ultimate desire that such a state of affairs exists. While I have argued that this is not in fact the case, it is a possible psychology.

Suppose, then, we narrow the question to this: Which kinds of psychological states of one's own are either the ultimate objects of or ultimate causes of our being motivated to bring about such states?

Given this question, if one says that what it *means* to say that a psychological state is pleasurable *is* that we are motivated to bring it about, sustain it, repeat it, and so on, then what we might call narrow psychological hedonism (hedonism with regard to that range of motivations) becomes a conceptual truth. *Of course* the only psychological states of one's own that are desired for their own sake are states of pleasure; their being desired *constitutes* their being states of pleasure.

But should that be a conceptual truth? Is it not a possible psychology—and indeed one defended by many—that there are psychological states we desire for their own sake but that are not states of pleasure, say the state of understanding a complex issue, or the state of believing in one's own integrity, or even the state of a completely nonhedonic contemplation of things? I argue that these are not actual psychologies, but they should not be ruled out a priori, as they would be if we define pleasure in terms of these relational properties. By contrast, if we define pleasure in terms of intrinsic qualities, we leave far more options open as empirical possibilities, and doing so is a theoretical advantage. It really should be an empirical question which kinds of psychological states we are motivated to sustain, repeat, and so on; more broadly, it should be an empirical question how pleasure is related to our other psychological states and what causal role it plays in our overall psychology.

I am not arguing that a theory that defines pleasure in terms of relational properties cannot be an empirical theory; but since such definitions are almost always made in terms of motivational states, there is a strong tendency for such theories to make narrow psychological hedonism a conceptual truth.

These points can be developed by considering some possible psychologies in which the various contingent causal connections postulated for Reward Events are severed and perhaps replaced by opposite connections. I will then resurvey the causal connections that, according to RET, constitute our actual psychology and note the various explanatory roles that can be played by such connections.

Before starting our tour, it may be mind broadening to be reminded of the history of curare. This drug was initially used in veterinary medicine and was thought to be a pain killer because when administered prior to surgery, the patients did not react to the surgery. A veterinarian then volunteered to undergo surgery with curare and afterward reported terrible pain. Curare, of course, does not stop pain; it only immobilizes.

The point here is that curare severs a set of standard causal connections between pain and certain bodily reactions. The pain is not constituted by those relational properties. Why might that not be the case for all relational properties with respect to both pain and pleasure?

PLEASURE AND COGNITION

Let us start first with contingent connections that do raise special puzzles when we try to construct a psychology in which they are severed. According to RET, pleasure is an affective state with no cognitive content. It follows that its connection with any cognitive state is a contingent (perhaps causal) connection; this contingency of connection is true even of introspective states, insofar as these are understood as second-order beliefs about or knowledge of our own internal psychological states. I have indeed assumed that we have reasonably accurate knowledge of the intrinsic qualities of states of pleasure, and I am inclined to believe the knowledge involves some causal connection between the pleasure (the state being introspected) and the belief about that state. But whatever the precise mechanism, what would it be like to scramble that mechanism, to sever the causal connections?

There is a preliminary question, however. Is pleasure (or pain) essentially a consciously experienced state? One's answer will depend on one's theory of consciousness.[2] I believe that the hedonic qualities of pleasure and displeasure are intrinsic qualities of our phenomenal experience and are thus consciously experienced as such; in that sense a creature could be aware of pleasure even though it had no cognitive state directed toward the pleasure. On the other hand, if any conscious experience, including the experience of pleasure, is in part *constituted by* introspection, then any conscious pleasure, though in one sense an affective state, would be essentially connected with cognition.

There is, nevertheless, something implausible about constituting a state by cognition of that very state. Such a relational-property theory threatens to collapse into an infinite regress: X is constituted by the knowledge of X. For now, I will assume that if felt affective states are always accompanied by introspection of those states, these are causal connections and thus could be severed. We are now in a position to sketch some strange counterpsychologies.

Let us imagine a creature who has psychological states with intrinsically positive hedonic tone but who systematically believes of such states that they are not pleasurable. There are several possibilities here.

Such a creature might be systematically confused about all his psychological states; none of his introspective beliefs about what he feels, believes, or wants would be at all accurate. Perhaps others can have knowledge of these states, and indeed perhaps our creature can have knowledge of the states of others and of himself by suitable application of theory, but introspection would play no role in supplying such knowledge. Indeed, the creature might learn to discount systematically his own spontaneous beliefs about his psychological states. Introspection and self-reflection, as evolved operations, would have to be seen as nonfunctional and perhaps even disadvantageous traits somehow linked to advantageous capacities in an evolutionary trade-off. This is, I think, a possible though very implausible psychology.

A less extreme possibility would be a creature that had reasonably accurate introspective knowledge of many of her psychological states—such as her beliefs, motives, and desires—but no such accurate knowledge of, or even beliefs about, the intrinsically positive (or negative) hedonic tone of her own experiences. The creature might experience intrinsically positive hedonic tone, but she would believe of all such experiences that they were not pleasurable, that they had no such quality.

This might be because the experience had, in addition to hedonic tone, a good deal of other content, from sensible qualities to intentional states, and the latter so dominated the creature's focus that she never developed distinct beliefs about hedonic quality as such. I have even suggested, in my exposition of RET, that cases of this kind are not unusual; the cases involve oversight, however, and not a systematic inability to focus on and have beliefs about hedonic tone.

Such systematic failure of belief is possible. If cognitive states are distinct from the objects of cognition, then it is possible for a creature to fail to develop the mechanisms for connecting cognition with the intrinsic qualities of experience. There is even the possibility of a creature who is capable of accurate introspection of intrinsic qualities, but who has such a strong theory-based belief that there are no intrinsic qualities in conscious experience—no qualia—that the creature not only fails to develop beliefs about the intrinsic qualities of his own experience but even develops the belief that the qualities are not there.[3]

RET claims that hedonic tone is a distinct, intrinsic, noncognitive quality of experience and that any connection between such qualities and cognition of those qualities is contingent. Introspection may be a distinct form of cognition, or more precisely a distinct method or mechanism for cognizing properties, but the connection between the mechanism and its objects is contingent.

PLEASURE AND MOTIVATION

Even if we allow that there could be a systematic disconnection between pleasure and cognitive states, we might still resist the possibility of there being such disconnection between pleasure and various motivational states. Surely a pleasant psychological state is a state one desires to continue, is motivated to obtain, and so forth; pleasure has a functional role to play and should be defined accordingly. In the next chapter, I examine Brandt's "relational property" theory of pleasure (1979), and later in this chapter I deal with the functional role issue in a discussion of levels of explanation in an empirical psychological hedonism. For now, I will sketch several possible psychologies that disconnect pleasure from motivation and desire.

First, consider an extreme version of the By-Product Theory discussed in chapter 2. On this theory, all ultimate motivation is directed toward or caused by various nonhedonic states (or beliefs about such states). Many of these states will be external to the agent, but some will be psychological states of the agent, such as states of knowledge (or beliefs that one has such knowledge). When one attains the desired state (or believes that one has attained it), this may cause pleasure, but this result is purely a by-product of the motivational machinery and plays no role either in the initial generation or in the sustaining of motivation. There is pleasure in the experience of a By-Product Theory creature, and it is pleasure because it is intrinsically positive, but it plays no causal role in motivation. As indicated earlier, this is a theory often defended with respect to many of our motivations, so it does not seem too wild a speculation to extend it to all motivation. I have argued that the theory is mistaken, but this is an empirical claim. But if being motivated to obtain or to sustain a psychological state thereby constitutes such a state as pleasurable, then once again narrow psychological hedonism is a priori true.

Some theorists do seem willing to accept this conclusion. For example, Edwards (1979) defends what he calls qualitative hedonism and claims that "the generic meaning of 'pleasure' is 'the set of all feelings we desire or wish to sustain or cultivate' " and that it is an "(analytically) true thesis that when pleasant feelings do occur, we do normally desire to sustain and repeat them" (95). It is a bit puzzling what the word 'normally' is doing in that last quotation, but this kind of approach often says that pleasure is not a quality of experience but an attitude toward or reaction to experiences, so that we would be safer to speak of "being pleased with . . ." rather than of "pleasure." I think this theory misses a very important quality of experience and also forecloses interesting empirical possibilities.

Consider, for example, a creature who experiences pleasure as an intrinsically positive quality but has strong beliefs that the intrinsically positive is to be avoided, that the life one ought to live would include no hedonic states, and so is thereby consistently motivated to avoid or to terminate all such states. (Are there not hints of Stoicism here?) Again, I do not believe such a psychology is a priori impossible.

It might be said, in reply, that if a psychological state is to count as pleasure, then the creature must enjoy the state, and that *is* to be motivated to sustain that state—to want the state to continue—and thus pleasure cannot be disconnected from all motivational states. This claim is, once again, an insistence on a relational-property theory of pleasure and a denial that pleasure is an intrinsic quality, which is precisely the point at issue. In addition, it misses a fundamental sense of 'enjoy.' To enjoy a psychological state, in the sense of finding it pleasant, is not to have some reaction to it, or some attitude toward it, or some motivation toward it; it is just to *be* in a psychological state that is intrinsically positive. It is far more a way of being than of doing. No intrinsic quality of experience is constituted by our reactions to that quality.

What this discussion points up is that much of the resistance to the view that pleasure is an intrinsic quality may simply be a corollary of a general resistance to any intrinsic phenomenal qualities. In addition, however, there may well be a sense that the intrinsically positive is perilously close to, say, G.E. Moore's "intrinsic goodness," a property, it is supposed, any naturalist should avoid. I deal more directly with that concern in the next chapter, when I argue that pleasure is indeed intrinsically good but that this does not have the normative implications often associated with that value term. It is the presumed normative implications that seem to support the claim that any naturalistic theory of value must commit the naturalistic fallacy.

Apart from value issues, someone might still argue that intrinsic phenomenal qualities would not have any explanatory role. If this objection is meant to focus on causal roles, then what I have been arguing is that this result is indeed a possibility, and one not to be ruled out a priori. The role of pleasure in our psychology is an empirical question, and understanding pleasure as an intrinsic quality can make clear why it is an empirical question.

There remain, however, important questions about explanation and functional roles. I can best deal with these by presenting a more systematic exposition of the various empirical claims made by RET.

PLEASURE AND EXPLANATION

In chapter 2, I sketched several possible creatures that would not be Reward Event Systems. Indeed, I believe there are many actual creatures that are not Reward Event Systems. Some of these are creatures whose behavior can be explained entirely in terms of wired-in reflexes; these creatures do not, perhaps, even have a psychology. Others probably have both informational states and motivational states that figure as differential causes of various types of behavior. The motivational states might, when present, produce a wired-in reaction to (informational states signaling the presence of) specific kinds of food, sex object, predator, and so on. But do such creatures learn to have new goals or to develop new objects of desire? Do they learn to avoid what they had initially pursued or to pursue what they had initially avoided? Perhaps they do, but the learning would require that experience of some new object (say by tasting it) reveals a quality of that object for which the creatures have wired-in motivations either to pursue or to avoid it. If that quality were different for each new kind of object, then there would have to be, correspondingly, that many different wired-in motivations.

The theorist who defines pleasure in terms of various motivational states directed toward a wide variety of experiences or objects thereby makes motivation radically pluralistic with respect to the causes or objects of the motivations. Such a relational-property theory of pleasure is analogous to many learning theories that define reward operationally in terms of the shaping of behavior. As I have argued, with such a conceptual move, reward no longer explains such learning; it only relabels it. So a relational-property conceptualization of pleasure does not explain a range of motivations; it simply relabels them.

I have speculated—and it is an empirical claim—that rather than having gone a radically pluralistic route, evolution solved the problem of flexibility and of learning new goals by developing Reward Event Systems. While these systems may have several motivations (as defined in chapter 2), the specific objects that become the focus of such motivation, and that the creature learns to pursue, have in common the ability to trigger Reward Events—an ability that in some cases may not have been there from the start but has developed through associative (Pavlovian) conditioning. When Reward Events are triggered, they play their role as intrinsic objects of motivation and as the ultimate causes of operant conditioning or of any learning of new goals. Such instances of intrinsically positive hedonic tone are, according to RET, the only qualities of experience that play that role. (In a full theory, an analogous but reverse role would be played by intrinsically negative hedonic tone.)

Let us pause for a moment at this evolutionary level of explanation. If we ask why Reward Events evolved, the answer will be either in terms of a function they perform or in terms of their being a genetically linked by-product of something functional. Ultimately, at the statistical level, the functions will be contributing to the survival and reproduction of the creatures with the genes for these more specific functions. What I have speculated is that Reward Events do play a functional role that has contributed to survival and reproduction via an economical solution to problems of learning and flexibility.

It might be said that I am thereby defining Reward Events functionally, but that charge would be true only in the sense that there is a generic evolutionary problem to be solved—a problem of providing creatures with positive motivations and with a capacity for selective learning. Creatures with multiple sensory contacts with the world are bombarded with signals; there needs to be filtering all along the line. In addition, there needs to be a way of determining what stored information will be utilized at any particular time. These needs could be seen, collectively, as problems of valencing potential information. Reward Events provide one possible solution, and as a monistic solution, it is in that sense very economical.

If, however, we do speculate on a monistic solution, wouldn't any event that played the roles assigned to Reward Events by RET thereby be, by definition, a Reward Event? This would be to treat 'Reward Event' as a term like 'Mendelian gene,' a theoretical term defined solely in terms of its function. Anyone of Mendel's time, and for a considerable time thereafter, had to define 'gene' this way since nothing else was known about whatever was producing those results.

No actual events, however, can be solely constituted by their functional roles or their relational properties. And it is often seen as progress in explanation to be able to specify the intrinsic properties of the events playing certain functional roles. There is something relatively unenlightening about being told that A is the cause of B, and that what we mean by 'A' is "the cause of B." At that stage of explanation, such a causal explanation is (by substitution) analytic: The cause of B is the cause of B. When we go on to find out some of the intrinsic properties of A, then our causal statement is both synthetic and potentially a good deal more informative. The scientific hope is that reference to the intrinsic qualities will become part of a theory specifying how the functions are performed, as has happened in genetic theory. And sometimes with such progress we may discover that A, now defined in terms of its intrinsic properties, does not play all the causal roles initially built into its functional definition. This is as it should be; for any object or event specified in terms of its intrinsic properties, it is an empirical question what causal relations it has to other events or objects.

RET characterizes pleasure as an intrinsic quality of experience and leaves it an empirical question what causal roles pleasure plays. I speculate that many of those who insist that pleasure should be defined functionally are influenced by their own sense of what is going on causally when they react to pleasure. The intrinsic quality that constitutes pleasure is intrinsically positive hedonic tone, but if, as RET claims, pleasure plays a central causal role, it would not be surprising if we thought of pleasure both in terms of its intrinsic quality and in terms of at least some of its causal roles. We might, indeed, find it very difficult to imagine the psychology of a creature that did not have our reactions to pleasure. This difficulty is a limitation of our imaginations, however, not a limitation on causal possibilities.

It may be difficult to make sense of such a counterpsychology, and we do have the notion that our psychological explanations should not only give us a causal story but should also rationalize behavior. Here I can only be brief and somewhat dogmatic. If explanations are in terms of causes, independently defined by their intrinsic properties, then such explanations will provide rational insight only in the sense that they may track the causal relations of our own psychology and thereby seem familiar or intuitively plausible. They are otherwise contingent causal truths. Indeed, whether the ultimate causal story of our own psychology will be intuitively plausible is an open question.

I have not claimed that the causal story postulated by RET is intuitively plausible. Many of the causal relations postulated by the theory are not open to introspection and are often not our primary focus in reflection.

There are forms of psychological hedonism that might try to remain more at the level of introspective phenomenology. For example, a version of the theory might say that the only ultimate cause of action is the belief that our action will sustain or bring about pleasure, perhaps coupled with a desire for pleasure as the only ultimate intentional object of desire. But this form of psychological hedonism is not RET. For one thing, both beliefs and desires are cognitive states—states with intentional content—and neither such states as a whole nor their intentional content are affective states. Pleasure is a noncognitive state of intrinsically positive hedonic tone. The thought of pleasure, or the desire for pleasure, is not itself a state of pleasure, though such thoughts or desires may be contingently associated with hedonic tone (positive or negative).

RET postulates that pleasure as such plays a distinctive causal role. The theory is to a degree modeled on conditioning theories (both Pavlovian and Skinnerian), but these theories can be interpreted in cognitive terms with beliefs and desires playing the central causal role. By contrast, RET speculates that while pleasure can be, and sometimes is, the conscious focus of belief and desire, much of the time it plays its causal role of periodic reinforcement in contexts in which beliefs and desires are focused on all sorts of other states, both internal and external. Only when such intentional states are rewarding, that is, only when they are associated in experience with positive hedonic tone, will motivation to pursue them be developed or sustained over time.

Much empirical detail is missing here. One can see RET as a quite generic theory with the species depending on the details of the relative roles of genetically determined connections with Reward Events, of connections brought about by some conditioning process, of beliefs that some activity will be rewarding, and so on.

What must be explained by any theory adequate to complex psychologies, human or nonhuman, is the development of new goals, including goals that are often seen by the individual as ends—as those things aimed at for their own sakes. The fundamental claim of RET is that all external goals, innate or learned, depend on an appropriate association with Reward Events, and that no external goal (innate or learned) ever becomes functionally autonomous, in the sense of continuing to be a goal in the absence of periodic reinforcement by Reward Events.

I will discuss a few of the possible interpretations of conditioning phenomena, both Pavlovian and operant, and indicate their implications with respect to the specific roles of Reward Events.[4]

REWARD EVENTS AND CONDITIONING

In Pavlovian conditioning, an unconditioned stimulus (US) produces an unconditioned response (UR), e.g., meat powder in a dog's mouth produces salivation. Then a conditioned stimulus (CS) is paired with (presented either prior to, prior to and simultaneous with, or simultaneous with) the US. (Backward conditioning, in which the CS is presented after the US, does not occur.) After a number of pairings, the CS by itself (say the sound of a bell) produces a conditioned response (CR) that is often quite similar to the UR but may differ in a number of details.

One of the debates among theorists is whether in Pavlovian conditioning the creature learns a direct association from CS to CR (what is called S-R learning) or whether what is learned is the association between CS and US (S-S learning). Note that the latter model invites a cognitive interpretation of the phenomenon—the creature learns to expect the US and this produces the anticipatory CR. (The dog salivates on hearing the bell, in expectation of the meat powder.)

Is there any reason for RET to favor one over the other of these options? Let us start with an unconditioned stimulus, that is, an experience or activity (say the tasting of saccharine by a rat) that innately triggers a Reward Event, the UR. Now pair with the US another activity or experience (the CS) so that over time the CS comes to trigger a Reward Event. According to the S-S explanation, our creature has learned to expect the US, and this expectation triggers anticipatory pleasure. By contrast, the S-R explanation suggests that the CS has become, in my terms, directly rewarding in a way that does not depend on cognitive expectation.

I have, in my discussions, tended to favor the latter interpretation, but a problem for RET (common to both versions of Pavlovian conditioning) is the phenomenon of *extinction*; if the CS continues to be presented, but the US is no longer presented, the CR ceases.

If the relevant response is the actual occurrence of a Reward Event, the implication would seem to be that an experience or activity cannot become directly rewarding on its own but must always remain dependent on being paired with whatever experiences innately trigger Reward Events. We could never learn to enjoy (find pleasure in) new kinds of activities, or rather our enjoyment of such activities could never become functionally autonomous from periodic pairing with an unconditioned source of pleasure.

I have argued against functional autonomy at a different level, in claiming that no external goals—or more precisely no desires for such external goals—ever become functionally autonomous in the sense that they would constitute a sustained motivation in the absence of periodic reinforcement by Reward Events. But this argument was not meant to deny the possibility that new kinds of experiences and activities could become directly rewarding, that is, become direct, functionally autonomous sources of Reward Events.

One could note that there are kinds of learned aversions, such as some kinds of phobias, which are notoriously resistant to extinction; the conditioned stimulus continues to cause, for example, fear, even though never thereafter paired with any naturally aversive stimulus. Some researchers speculate that this resistance to extinction may be due to the Pavlovian conditioning taking place in a very young organism with an immature nervous system, which makes the conditioning "context independent and resistant to extinction" (Schwartz 1989, 132). If we were to apply such a model to learned sources of pleasure, it would seem to require that they be learned at an early age, and this requirement does not seem promising as an account of sophisticated, adult human sources of pleasure.

On the other hand, at this stage, any theory should be open to theoretical speculation and empirical evidence. Might it be the case that all sources of pleasure for a species or individual have some general properties in common, properties that are innate triggers of Reward Events? Or can new brain circuitry become a direct causal source of Reward Events in a way that is not dependent on being paired periodically with causal sources that are wired in innately? And if this can happen, how does it happen? Does Pavlovian conditioning, with an appropriate handling of the issue of extinction, give the right model?

These are difficult and important questions, to which I do not have answers. What needs to be explained by any theory is not only the development of new goals but also the loss of old goals. Not only do new experiences and activities become rewarding, old experiences and activities cease to be. The general neurological speculation of RET is that somehow the neural circuitry underlying these experiences and activities can both causally connect with and be disconnected from the Reward Event circuitry. Indeed, since many kinds of activities (e.g., eating) are periodically rewarding and nonrewarding (satiation), the machinery had better allow for quite dynamic processes of change. Just how this happens remains to be determined. It could involve processes that do not follow the laws of Pavlovian conditioning.

The other major role for Reward Events in RET is as the internal reward underlying operant conditioning. A typical description of this area of study is as follows:

> The study of operant conditioning is the study of how contingencies of reward and punishment influence the future likelihood of the behavior that produces them. The law of effect tells us that responses that produce positive consequences (reinforcement), or eliminate (escape) or prevent (avoidance) negative consequences, will increase in frequency. Responses that produce negative consequences, or prevent positive ones, will be decreased in frequency (punishment). (Schwartz 1989, 181)

We should note how easy it is, in interpreting this passage, to slide between a causal interpretation and an analytic interpretation. If it is an empirical law that positive consequences cause an increase in frequency of the behavior, then we need a characterization of reward that is independent of these behavioral consequences; RET provides such a characterization by defining a Reward Event as an event with intrinsically positive hedonic tone. This is the point I stressed in my discussion of Wise in chapter 2.

Thus, when the question is raised, "What makes an event a reinforcer?" (Schwartz 1989, 182), if the events referred to are externally characterized activities (drinking, eating, etc.), the answer of RET is that these events must trigger Reward Events. That the Reward Events themselves are reinforcers (that is, do have the operant conditioning behavioral effects) is a fundamental causal claim of RET.

On the question raised earlier, in our discussion of Pavlovian conditioning, of whether new activities can become functionally autonomous sources of Reward Events, Schwartz suggests a negative answer when he says, "Critical to establishing a conditioned reinforcer is that it provide information about the unconditioned reinforcer. . . . To be a conditioned reinforcer a stimulus must not only provide information, but it must provide good information; that is, it must be associated with a positive unconditioned reinforcer" (183). If by "associated with" is meant "*continues* to be periodically associated with," then this is a denial of functional autonomy for the conditioned reinforcer, analogous to the claim that a conditioned stimulus must continue to be periodically paired with the unconditioned stimulus or the conditioned response will extinguish.

On the other hand, in a discussion of the role of token rewards in operant conditioning, as when chimpanzees are trained to respond operantly for tokens that they can cash in only infrequently for food, Schwartz notes that such conditioned reinforcers serve a variety of functions. Some of these are primarily informational (providing feedback that one has done the right thing, telling the organism what to do next, and bridging long periods between unconditioned reinforcers), but he also suggests that "conditioned reinforcers may have hedonic functions. It may feel good to obtain them in the way it feels good to obtain food" (180-81). This leaves us with our Pavlovian question: How do new objects, events, or activities become direct, functionally autonomous sources of Reward Events (assuming that they do)?

Apart from these questions concerning conditioned reinforcers (rewards), there remains the question of how an unconditioned reward works in operant conditioning. In the terms of RET, how do Reward Events cause creatures to come to engage in those learned activities that produce such Reward Events?

I shall focus on just one specific question, which I have already raised in my discussion of Reward Event Systems. If an activity has produced Reward Events, and then in new circumstances that again make such activity possible, the creature repeats the activity, or even seeks out the circumstances for the activity, is this solely because the creature expects, that is, believes, that the activity will be pleasurable, and this, coupled with a desire for pleasure, produces the behavior? Or must the thought of the activity itself trigger a degree of hedonic tone in order for the creature to be motivated to engage in the activity? These are both empirical possibilities.

There do seem to be cases when a belief that an activity will be pleasurable does not get someone to take the needed steps to engage in the activity, or a belief that an experience will be aversive does not get someone to take the needed steps to avoid that experience. (Some of the cases discussed by Damasio [1994] fit this description; the individuals lack "practical reason.") Sometimes it is said that the beliefs must be "vivid" (see Brandt 1979), but this claim is vague and the situation might better be explained by the failure of the beliefs to trigger any present hedonic tone (positive or negative). In addition, there are cases where the focus of motivation is the bringing about of a state of affairs the agent does not expect to experience at all. Here, an RET explanation does seem to require that the thought of, or the envisaging of, the outcome be able to trigger present Reward Events.

It might be asked why, if the thought itself triggers Reward Events, the creature would bother to act. Here we no doubt do need some cognitive expectation and some ability to compare the degree of positive affect triggered by the thought of the activity and the (presumably) higher degree of positive affect triggered by the activity itself. We should remember, however, that people do sometimes get caught up in fantasy. In addition, there could be a role for the present aversiveness (negative hedonic tone) of the thought that one does not yet have a desired goal—and so on.

Many of these empirical possibilities are consistent with RET. What the theory must insist on is that the *thought* of positive affect (a psychological state with that intentional content) is not in itself an *instance* of positive affect, and that it is actual instances that play a key causal role in explaining behavior, including learned behavior. Wherever well-established learning theory assigns a causal role to reward, RET makes the empirical claim that it is internal, affective Reward Events that are playing that role.

Recent surveys of the neurology of reinforcement can be interpreted as being consistent with the general empirical shape of RET. For example, a volume on *Models of Information Processing in the Basal Ganglia* (Houk et al. 1994) has a section on "Reward Mechanisms." The focus is on positive reinforcement in learning theory. This focus is initially psychological, but the aim is to provide neurological explanations for well-established psychological phenomena. Wickens and Kötter, in their article "Cellular Models of Reinforcement" (187-214), accept as the basic psychological data that "the effect of reinforcement (satisfaction) is to strengthen the association between the situation and the act. This formulation implicitly requires a mechanism capable of integrating *three* factors (presynaptic and postsynaptic activity, and neurochemical reinforcement)" (187, my emphasis).

The assumption being made by Wickens and Kötter is that in addition to the situation (environmental stimuli) and the action, there is a distinct internal factor that causes situations and actions to be associated in operant conditioning. Even when the relevant factors are all internalized in the brain, there is still a "three-factor rule" that connects pre- and post-synaptic activity with reward (see 194).

RET, of course, finds most congenial the labeling of this third factor as satisfaction (the term used by Thorndike [1911] when he first formulated the "law of effect"), but Wickens and Kötter aim "to translate the psychological concept of positive reinforcement into physiological actions of dopamine" (188). There is already, in this statement, an ambiguity that goes beyond the issue of psychological versus neurological explanations. RET claims that the actions of (probably) dopamine underlie (a deliberately noncommittal term) satisfaction—a distinct quality of positive hedonic tone—and that it is this psychological/neurological event that causes a strengthening of the pre- and post-synaptic connections (and ultimately the associations of situations and actions). Wickens and Kötter, however, refer to positive reinforcement; that label seems more appropriate for the strengthening of associations rather than for the "third-factor" cause of the strengthening. The ambiguity runs throughout the article, as the terms 'reinforcement' and 'satisfaction' tend to be seen as equivalent.

The articles in the "Reward Mechanisms" section survey a growing body of evidence for the central role of dopamine in reward phenomena. Schultz et al. (233-48) note that "the major stimuli for dopamine neurons are reward-related events, both primary rewards and conditioned, reward-producing stimuli" (236). They also note that "the dopamine responses do not encode the particular physical properties of the eliciting event; both primary rewards and conditioned stimuli with differing sensory characteristics elicit a *common dopamine response*" (237, my emphasis). It requires an interpretive leap, but this statement is at least consistent with RET's claim that intrinsic reward is a distinct aspect of experience, separate from any cognitive or informational content.

The "Reward Mechanisms" articles also provide some interesting hypotheses about how, at the neurological level, positive reinforcement works. The hypotheses attempt to account for a wide variety of conditioning phenomena. Whether this meeting of psychology and neurology prefigures a replacement of the former by the latter can be left an open question, though I believe such an outcome is implausible. At a minimum, psychology provides the data for the neurological hypotheses about the underlying mechanisms for psychological phenomena. It thus will continue to be important that we characterize psychological phenomena in ways that do not leave out aspects that can turn out to be theoretically important at both the psychological and neurological level. It is a central thesis of RET that pleasure—positive hedonic tone—is just such an aspect; it is a third factor with its own intrinsic qualities.

The basic claims of RET, as a theory of motivation, are empirical claims about the contingent, causal connections between pleasure and other psychological states. I think psychological hedonism—even in its narrow form as a claim about which of our own psychological states can function as ultimate, functionally autonomous causes of motivation and desire—should be empirical. And I think it can be, since we do have a way of identifying pleasure in terms of its intrinsic quality of positive hedonic tone. That characterization of pleasure has the advantage not only of being an accurate description of experiences of pleasure but also of leaving open a wide range of empirical possibilities about the role of pleasure in our psychology.

SUMMARY

RET claims that Reward Events are both intrinsically positive (in the sense that this describes an intrinsic quality of such events) and intrinsically motivating (in the somewhat different sense that they are motivating—a relational property—in their own right, and with no dependence on periodic connection with other kinds of events). Indeed, in its theory of motivation, RET makes the bold claim that in those creatures that are Reward Event Systems (which includes us and a considerable range of other creatures), only Reward Events are intrinsically (positively) motivating. (Aversion events, characterized in terms of intrinsically negative hedonic tone, would correspondingly be the only events that are intrinsically negatively motivating; positive and negative motivation would be characterized in terms of, respectively, tendencies to seek or to avoid.) This claim is supported by a growing body of neuropsychological evidence, but of course it remains vulnerable to counterevidence, as should any psychological theory that claims to explain how we work.

In addition, I have argued for the advantages, with respect to psychological theory, of conceptualizing Reward Events in terms of an intrinsic quality of experience that is positive in its own right, has no cognitive content, and is only contingently connected with either cognition or motivation.

There are, I will now argue, further advantages to a theory that characterizes key psychological events as being both intrinsically motivating and intrinsically positive. These dual characteristics provide the empirical/theoretical basis for a naturalistic theory of intrinsic value.

4

NATURALIZING VALUE

What, if anything, has intrinsic value? We need to make several conceptual distinctions before we can make use of the empirical/theoretical claims of the Reward Event Theory of motivation in answering this question. First, there can be much disagreement about what makes a philosophical theory naturalistic. What is it to naturalize value, or the mental, or any other contested concept? Second, is there any way of specifying at the beginning what counts as value, without begging all the questions? 'Value' is a notoriously slippery term.[1] There is a good deal of ideology involved in specifications of the function of value. I argue for a purified concept in which intrinsic value is not normative. I need, therefore, to defend my view against a critic who may say, "Well, whatever you have naturalized, it isn't *value*."

What I argue is that positive hedonic tone (pleasure) is a natural, intrinsic (nonrelational) property that is intrinsically good, that it is (probably) the only natural property that is intrinsically good, and that the presence of this property in the experience of a creature is what makes life worth living *for that creature*. Such intrinsic goodness, I argue, has no definitional or perhaps even obvious connection with norms, morality, what we ought to do, or even what we have reason to do. There is no naturalistic fallacy involved in naturalizing intrinsic value. Separating the intrinsically good from the normative does not remove it from the realm of value, but rather frees it from assumptions that prevent our seeing it for the natural property it is.

For now, I say only that I am on the track of the intrinsically good, that which is good *in its own right*, without going on to say (as is common) that the intrinsically good is the desir*able*, or is *worthy* of being desired.

NATURALISTIC CONSTRAINTS, PLAUSIBILITY AND EMPIRICAL PSYCHOLOGY

Any current scientific theory counts as naturalistic, and thus any entities or properties postulated in such theories will also be natural. Any entities or properties postulated by any philosophical theory will also count as natural if they are identical with, or are constituted by, or are supervenient upon scientific properties, provided that the identity, or constitution, or supervenience is no more problematical than the corresponding relations between properties postulated in the social sciences and psychology, and those in biology, neurology, and physics.[2]

Even with this rather relaxed set of requirements for a naturalistic theory, a naturalist might well believe that the most defensible view is that goodness is not a real property at all. Such a nonrealist will either explain our use of value terms as having a function other than that of ascribing a property (such as prescribing, or commending), or else admit that our language involves such realistic claims but argue that these claims are all false (as in Mackie's 1977 "error theory").

A realist will hold that such properties exist. A theory must then decide whether value properties are intrinsic properties or relational properties. An intrinsic property of some x is a property that x has in its own right, independent of its relations to some y or z or to some wider context. By contrast, a relational property of x is constituted by such relations. Thus, being square would be an intrinsic property of x, while being between-y-and-z would be a relational property of x. It should be noted that both intrinsic and relational properties are equally real, objective, or nonrelative. If x is between y and z, this is a fact about x, and the statement that x is between y and z is true, not "true for some and not for others," much less "true for x."

A realist theory must also explain what it is for a property to be a *value* property. Different conceptions of value will put different constraints on possible theories.

Finally, a realist must deal with a series of interconnected theoretical questions: How do we gain knowledge of (reasonable belief about) value properties? How does this knowledge compare with our knowledge of nonvalue properties? What role do properties of intrinsic value and disvalue play in our overall psychology? How are they related to motivation? Is this role compatible with the findings of empirical psychology? Can the theory of intrinsic value be seen as part of an overall naturalistic picture?

A minimal naturalistic constraint on a philosophical theory is that if such a theory makes any causal claims—say claims about how humans are motivated—then those claims should be consistent with an existing scientific theory or it should be reasonably clear how the claims could be tested empirically and could eventually become part of a scientific theory.

What is the relevance of this constraint to a theory of value? Let me state a plausibility constraint on any such theory, which must also be a minimal constraint, since otherwise it would beg too many questions right at the start. The constraint is that any theory of positive intrinsic value—the intrinsically good—should be able to show that human beings, and probably other sentient creatures, are at least sometimes motivated to try to obtain that good for its own sake. (A corresponding constraint would be stated for negative intrinsic value—the intrinsically bad—and motivation to try to avoid that bad.) In other words, a theory must count as *implausible* if it identifies as the good something that no human, perhaps even no sentient being, has ever been motivated to try to obtain for its own sake.[3]

If a naturalistic theory, which is also realist about value, meets this plausibility constraint, then it must say that at least sometimes intrinsic value plays a causal role in human motivation, and it then becomes subject to the minimal naturalistic constraint. The theory must show how intrinsic value can play this role in our psychology and how that role is compatible with empirical psychological theories.

PROBLEMS FOR INTRINSIC VALUE AS A NONPSYCHOLOGICAL INTRINSIC PROPERTY

Suppose a theorist wishes to meet the constraints and is sympathetic to the pluralistic view that a number of different things have intrinsic value and that at least some of these things are not psychological states. Finally, suppose the theorist assumes that the primary categories of an adequate psychological theory are cognition and conation, so that such a theory parallels the fairly standard belief/desire theory appealed to by many philosophers. What sort of realist theory of value might come out?

First, consider an x that is neither a psychological state nor some other state of a sentient organism—say a work of art or a bit of nature. What would it be for x to be intrinsically good? Might this goodness be an intrinsic property of x? The idea that value properties are out there, and could exist in a world uninhabited by any sentient being might seem to strain even the most tolerant naturalism. How might such a value property play a role in human motivation?

Working with the belief/desire model, a theory could say that a person must first have genuine cognition of the property. The weaker claim—that the person need only have a belief that x is good—does not make a compelling case for the goodness itself playing a role in motivation, since a belief that p can play a psychological role independent of whether p is true.

We are now in the territory of Mackie's much debated "argument from queerness" that if there were objective values, "they would be entities or qualities or relations of a very strange sort, utterly different from anything else in the universe" (1977, 38).

This is a double charge, summed up in the claim that such objective value would have to be "authoritatively prescriptive." In part, according to Mackie, to be aware of such authoritative prescriptivity would be to be aware "of the truth of these distinctively ethical [value] premises" (39). In terms of our example, this awareness would require genuine cognition of the intrinsic goodness of x as an intrinsic property of x, and poses the epistemological problem of how such cognition is possible and whether it can be seen as part of an overall naturalistic theory of cognition. If the problem were only the general difficulty of explaining how we come to know any intrinsic properties of an external x, this would not be a special problem for value properties. But the deeper problem is to explain what it is for a property to be a value property. According to Mackie, a value property must be both authoritative and prescriptive:

> something's being good both tells the person who knows this to pursue it and makes him pursue it. An objective good would be sought by anyone who was acquainted with it, not because of any contingent fact that this person, or every person, is so constituted that he desires this end, but just because the end has to-be-pursuedness somehow built into it. (40)

Critics of Mackie have often charged him with begging the question in favor of internalism as opposed to externalism. These terms have been used in various ways, but the general idea is that for an internalist there is an internal, conceptual link between being a (positive) value and motivating pursuit; it cannot be merely a *contingent fact* that humans (and perhaps other sentient beings) are motivated to pursue the good.

How might assuming internalism beg the question against the view we have been considering—that goodness is an intrinsic property of an external x? A defender of the view might say that Mackie blurs the distinction between cognition and motivation—that our primary contact with the good is cognitive, that is, we come to know that x is intrinsically good. Whether we are then motivated to pursue the good must depend on contingent facts about us, although it may be the case that in many people cognition of the good causes desire for the good or motivation to pursue the good.

Fair enough. That the connection between value and motivation may be only a contingent connection is a possible view, and, indeed, I argue that it is the truth of the matter. If, however, an intrinsic property is not a value property because (conceptually) it is linked to motivation, what does make it a value property? Should we accept Mackie's background assumption that the good must somehow tell us what to do?

I will return to these questions. For now, I can say that if intrinsic value is an intrinsic property of an x, a property that is not itself a motivational state, then the connection between value and motivation must be contingent. The question then arises, generated by the constraints, as to how cognition of goodness relates to motivation. Is it that cognition of the goodness of x directly causes motivation to pursue x? Is there any psychological evidence, with respect to any other properties, for such direct motivation by cognition, or is the psychological role of goodness sui generis? Would it be plausible to see the reaction to goodness as analogous to such reflex actions as ducking when a brick is thrown at us? These questions do not raise insuperable problems, but they suggest why it has seemed to many naturalists that a theory of intrinsic value as an intrinsic property generates more problems than it solves.

Mackie, of course, thought that one should just abandon any realism or objectivity about value and admit that all there are in the universe are various natural nonvalue properties and our various psychological reactions to those properties. But is there not another possibility? Might not value properties *be* relational properties? Why not say that for x to have intrinsic value is for it to stand in certain (appropriate) relations to our psychological states, particularly our motivations or desires? There may be a mild paradox in claiming that intrinsic value is a relational property, but this position is otherwise a quite proper realism. As emphasized earlier, relational properties are just as real as intrinsic properties. It can be a perfectly objective truth that some x has a relational property.

This point has been obscured by a tendency to assume that if the relation involves subjective, psychological states, the relational property is thereby subjective in a sense that tells against objectivity and realism. But this assumption is a confusion. The issue is not whether relational properties are real properties but whether intrinsic value is constituted by some such relational properties, particularly by those involving psychological states.

There are many possible variations to relational-property theories, and I will not be examining each of these in detail. I instead divide such theories into two general types, which I call epistemological and ontological, and I then argue that only the ontological theories give us a genuine theory of value. I then go on to indicate problems raised by ontological theories; finally, I outline an alternative intrinsic-property theory and argue that this theory has advantages, as a realism that can meet the naturalistic constraints.

Types of Psychological/Relational Theories of Value

First, a reminder of an earlier assumption: We are examining theories that accept some variant of a belief/desire model for human psychology. Thus, the psychological states appealed to in a relational property theory will be (roughly) either cognitive or conative.

A cognitive-based theory would have the following general form: x is intrinsically good if, and only if, a suitably specified subject in suitably specified circumstances would judge that (or come to believe that) x is intrinsically good.

Could a theory of this type be a theory about what constitutes the goodness of x? This is prima facie implausible. If to be intrinsically good is to be judged intrinsically good, then what is the content of that judgment? One would have to judge or come to believe that x is judged to be intrinsically good. But this judgment still does not provide a content for the primary judgment. The theory would seem to be involved in an infinite regress. Nor is this difficulty resolved by substituting the stronger cognitive state of knowledge for that of belief. It would be an odd realism that would say that x's being F is constituted by some subject's knowing that x is F.

Such cognition-based theories should be seen as epistemological, not ontological. In specifying conditions for the subject and the situation, the theory is specifying conditions that are likely to generate accurate judgment that x is good. It would not seem enough merely to specify conditions that generate belief that x is good. All sorts of conditions can generate the belief that x is F; specifying these conditions does not tell us much about whether x *is F*, much less what sort of property F is.

Of course, sufficient constraints on conditions of knowing could put some constraints on what sort of property F is, but prima facie such a theory would seem to be compatible with both intrinsic-property and relational-property theories. The key point, however, is that a theory about how we come to know that x is F is not the same as a theory about the nature of F. And that is what we wanted.

If a relational-property theory does not make cognition constitutive of value, then given the assumption of a belief/desire psychology, the constitutive properties must be conative—desire, motivation, preference, etc. This claim is a bit overstated—such theories do characteristically bring cognition back into the picture as a constraint on desire—but the key to value is seen to lie in this more dynamic side of our psychology.

This is a promising move. Constituting value in terms of motivation can provide a conceptual connection between value and the ability to motivate sentient creatures, thereby meeting the plausibility constraint. And if the belief/desire model of the causes of action is seen as the basic form of current empirical psychological theories, a value theory that accepts this model could meet the minimal naturalistic constraint. Furthermore, such a theory promises to allow for a considerable pluralism with respect to the objects of value—the objects that have the relational property of intrinsic goodness; for many, this kind of pluralism is far more plausible than any monistic theory of value.

Of course, there are difficulties and disagreements. Many defenders of such theories do not see themselves as defending an objective, realist theory of value. Thus, Gauthier (1986) says, "Desire, not thought, and volition, not cognition, are the springs of good and evil" (21). He then goes on to claim that "although values are ascribed to states of affairs, the ascription is attitudinal, not observational, subjective, not objective. . . . Thus the theory of rational choice treats value as a subjective and relative measure, not an objective and absolute standard" (25). But as we have seen, it can be a perfectly objective, nonrelative fact that some x has a relational property, even if that property involves a relation to a subjective, psychological state. Nevertheless, many realists might not be satisfied with this sort of objective, relational property, because they could not see such properties playing the roles they believe should be played by value, such as helping to resolve disputes.

To illustrate this point, a very ecumenical form of the theory might say that for x to have intrinsic value is for x to be "any object of any interest." On such a view, any given x might have value for A and not for B or might have positive value for A and negative value for B. This situation might not help A and B to resolve a dispute as to whether, as a common enterprise, they should pursue x, or even whether x should be pursued by anyone.

Few current forms of relational-property realism are that ecumenical. Most, for varying reasons, put different constraints on desire or preference before it can count as the basis of value. Even Gauthier, who does not see his theory as objective, insists that preferences must be "coherent and considered" if they are to constitute the value that can "play normative roles in the framework for understanding human action afforded by the theory of rational choice" (27).

In brief, the constraints placed on the conative properties that constitute value are often generated by theoretical assumptions about what it is for a property to be a value property. For many, value plays a key role in directing choice or in guiding our reflections on how to live; it functions in a context of what are seen as paradigmatically human rational activities. Thus, cognition is reintroduced as a constraint on desire. Desires are to be "informed," or are to survive "cognitive psychotherapy," and so forth.

Reintroducing cognition in this way need not generate the regress problems noted earlier in cognitive-relational theories, as long as the relevant knowledge, or reasonable belief, or whatever is of nonvalue properties or states of affairs. It is not really a plausible constraint on a relational-property theory grounded in conation to say, for example, that x has value if x is desired, but only if that desire is informed by (generated by?) the knowledge that x is good. The theory should claim that x is good because it is desired (under appropriate constraints), not that x is desired because it is good.

A theorist might object, however, to too severe a constraint on introducing anything normative into the conditions constituting value. A realist, she might say, need not be committed to reductive naturalism, in which all value is defined in terms of nonvalue properties. Thus, someone might suppose that we have a more perspicuous grasp of norms in the sphere of rationality, and that we can use a concept of rationality in our characterization of the good.

Even here, however, naturalistic constraints have force. If one characterizes reasons or rationality in a strongly normative way (how we *ought* to reason, and so on), and if one claims that a person's reasons help explain her actions, one needs to develop a model of how these reasons cause action. Can cognition as such (knowledge, reasonable belief) directly cause action? Few psychological theories support this, and so it is not surprising that a view of reasons for action as a combination of belief and desire remains a dominant model.

If, then, our conative side must be brought into the picture in order to explain how belief generates action, and if value is seen as being essentially practical, there could be even further incentive for making practical effect an essential part of what it is for a property to be a value property. And the most perspicuous way to do that would seem to be to make such value a relational property, relating some x to motivation or desire, seen as that in us which moves us to action.

Theories of this type must somehow bring together both the actual causal role of value and its normative or directive role; assumptions about the latter role tend to determine the conditions placed on desire before it is to count as constituting value.

While different conative-relational-property theories will have their specific advantages and difficulties, we can note certain generic advantages. By building in a tie to motivation, they meet the plausibility constraint. (But a note of caution: If in meeting its conception of the normative, or of the role of value, a theory puts too many or too idealized constraints on desire, it could make it less and less plausible that any actual human—or any nonhuman animal—ever met those conditions and so was ever in fact motivated in the "proper" way.) In their models of actual motivation, they need appeal only to cognition of (or belief about) natural, nonvalue facts and motivations directed toward natural states of affairs, and this position would meet our naturalistic constraint (on the assumption that empirical psychological theories will at least in outline be of the belief/desire form). Finally, there appears to be ample room for a pluralism of intrinsic values. While the relational property constituting intrinsic value is (presumably) the same in all cases,[4] the things that have such intrinsic value can be as various as the professed goals of humans (or reflective humans) or the objects endorsed by "our" intuitions.

We should note, however, that relational property theories are in an important sense no more pluralistic than intrinsic property theories. Just as the relational property can be true of a wide variety of objects, so an intrinsic quality can be associated with an equal variety of experiences.

Finally, we can note a major theoretical problem for any relational property theory of value in which the relevant relations have to do with desires, preferences, or motivations. The problem (clearly identified by Brandt 1979, 247-53) has to do with whether it can make any conceptual sense to maximize such value over the lifetime of a creature, particularly if the creature changes preferences over time (a very common state of affairs in human beings). These maximization problems for preference theories of value will be discussed later in more detail.

For now, rather than argue directly against such relational-property theories of value, I will sketch an alternative intrinsic-property theory and then focus on the key disagreements. Some of these disagreements are empirical: about what in fact the central causes of behavior are and about whether an adequate psychological theory needs to go beyond the belief/desire model. Other disagreements are more traditionally philosophical: about how intrinsic value is related to the normative and about what it means to say that something is normative.

Intrinsic Value as an Intrinsic Property

The Reward Event Theory claims that intrinsic (positive) value is an intrinsic property of certain psychological states; specifically, it is the property of positive affect or hedonic tone. This positive hedonic tone is distinct from, and can vary independent of, any other properties or contents of experience. Positive affect (pleasure) does not itself have any propositional content; to experience such affect is not, in itself, to be in any propositional-attitude state. Particular instances of pleasure are what I have called Reward Events.

This theory is a version of value hedonism, a version partially structured by the theory of motivation outlined in chapters 2 and 3. According to RET, Reward Events provide a vital contingent connection between motivational states, cognitive states, and various actions. It is claimed that actions, and desires directed toward the goals of such actions, will be sustained over time if and only if these actions trigger in the appropriate way Reward Events in the brain. The appropriate way is to be determined empirically, e.g., by evidence of the effectiveness of varying schedules of reinforcement. The theory does not assume a priori that reward on every trial is most effective in sustaining motivation (and indeed, the empirical evidence suggests otherwise).

It should be emphasized again that RET insists that Reward Events are *intrinsically* rewarding, and that this is a fact separate from and only contingently connected with their role in shaping behavior. Furthermore, the positive affect of Reward Events has no propositional content. If these events play a key causal role, then any theory emphasizing only psychological states with propositional content (belief/cognition, desire/conation) lacks a key causal piece.

There is a further distinction made by RET that is both empirically and philosophically important. This is the distinction, discussed earlier, between the focus and the anchor of desire. In creatures complex enough to have states with intentional content, desires generally will be focused on external goals and on activities related to those goals: food (or the eating of food), significant others (or mating with same), or whales (and the saving of same). And since there may be no other intentional content in focus, it may be assumed that the objects of that content are the ultimate aims of the creature, that these are the things desired for their own sake, and that they thus provide (along with appropriate beliefs) the causal explanation of actions.

By contrast, RET claims that the key causal role is the triggering of Reward Events. These are the real anchor of ongoing motivation or desire and *in that sense* could be said to be the only things desired for their own sake. This distinction applies not only to complex human motivations but also to primary motivations such as hunger or primary rewards such as the eating of food. Nevertheless, one can plausibly speculate that a Reward Event mechanism no doubt evolved to keep creatures focused on and willing to work for those external goals essential to biological success. But the real reward is internal, affective, and only contingently connected with other goals.

Someone might grant all the above empirical facts and nevertheless reject the conclusion about intrinsic value—about what is valued for its own sake. This would seem to be the position taken by Brandt (1979), who develops a theory of the good based on extensive use of conditioning theory. While this is not as neurological a base as RET employs, it is certainly consistent with such further grounding of conditioning phenomena. Brandt says:

> To say that something is wanted for itself is not, of course, to say that its being so is 'functionally autonomous' in the sense that its status will persist without occasional 'reinforcements' in the sense of support, say, by occasional gratifications from experience with the valenced entity or situations like it (32).

Surely, however, functional autonomy *is* the issue. If something never can function independently, on its own, as either the object of motivation or as a reinforcement for motivation,[5] it is not persuasive to say that it is nevertheless desired for its own sake. The reply might be that if something does not require *constant* reinforcement for it to be motivating, then that is sufficient for it to be wanted for itself. The empirical evidence indicates, however, that motivation is sustained most effectively through periodic reinforcement, and in that sense periodic reinforcement *is* how motivation is dependent on reinforcement. Thus, if the best psychological theories tell us that A (e.g., wanting some kind of food) is dependent on the differential causal operation of B (e.g., periodic reinforcement by Reward Events), and that even eating the food is not itself a consummatory experience (is not, in my terms, an intrinsically positive experience) but can at most trigger experience of a Reward Event, then a plausible naturalistic theory of value should not say either that the food (or even eating the food) is wanted for its own sake or that it is intrinsically rewarding.[6]

In this context, it is important to keep in mind the psychological difference between a deliberate, conscious means-end stance ("You are doing A for the sake of B") and a causal grounding in something on which we are not focused ("You are only pursuing goal G because of the causal work of Reward Events"). The "because" of RET is *not* the "because" of deliberative practical reasoning.[7]

A critic might still insist, however, that wanting or desire is necessarily a state with intentional content, that it must have a focus. Thus, even if an additional aspect of experience (e.g., positive hedonic tone) is playing a causal role, this is no reason to make that hedonic tone the intentional object of desire, particularly if positive affect need not be present in all cases of desire or motivation (assuming motivation is sustained with only periodic reinforcement). The conclusion then would be that if one desires x and does not desire x for the sake of a further intentional object y, then it is indeed x that one desires for its own sake, no matter how this desire is causally dependent on other aspects of experience that are not the intentional object of desire.

In reply, the first point to note is that pleasure (intrinsically positive hedonic tone) can be an intentional object; it can be the focus of an experience and reported as such, as is the case in many introspective reports in the psychological literature. This fact would be denied by those who defend a theory that says that pleasure is a relational property—some attitude toward a further content of experience; I have already argued against such theories and for a theory of pleasure as an intrinsic quality, and I will have more to say on this issue later in this chapter.

Second, as the criticism stands, it seems to assume that if a creature desires x for its own sake, that is sufficient to constitute x as an intrinsic value for that creature, thereby creating an *instance* of intrinsic value in the life of that creature. But that position cannot be quite right. Having a desire for x for its own sake, or a preference for x (even a reflective or considered preference), does not as such bring intrinsic value into the life of a creature. Otherwise having a large number of unfulfilled desires would be the key to the good life.

Surely, at a minimum, if one desires (for its own sake) that x be the case, x must *be* the case if there is to be an actual instance of intrinsic value. And is even that state of affairs sufficient? If a person desires that x be the case, and her desire is satisfied in only the minimal sense that x *is* the case, but she never *knows* that it is the case, does this create an instance of intrinsic value that increases the intrinsic value of her life *for her*? Some philosophers would defend this possibility of unknown benefits and harms (see Nagel 1986), but there is an implausibility to such positions, perhaps particularly for any naturalistic theory. How, after all, could such value, if constituted by the coming into existence of a state of affairs that has no impact on the psychology of the individual, play any role in actual motivations? Granted, preferences or desires can play such a role, but once again it is not the desiring of x as such, whether fulfilled or not, that can really constitute an instance of intrinsic value.

Would it be sufficient, then, if the person who desires x for its own sake comes to experience that x is the case? But there is the all-too-common experience of someone wanting x, perhaps very strongly and for a very long time, and then, on getting x, not finding it at all satisfactory. In the minimal sense of the coming into existence of the object of desire, her desire is satisfied, but *she* is not, and surely it is the latter satisfaction that is the key to intrinsic value. It is the lived quality of experience—its intrinsically positive hedonic tone—that is the key to intrinsic value. This is a quality of experience that we discover, and the discovery is often at odds with what we had desired.

In addition, if RET's psychological theory is correct, such discoveries—such actual instances of hedonic tone—are the key to creating new desires, to sustaining desire over time, and to constituting an experience that is satisfactory in its own right. For all these reasons, while it may well be something of a departure from our everyday talk of what we desire for its own sake, there is a good theoretical case for saying that insofar as desiring for its own sake is relevant to intrinsic value, only positive hedonic tone is desired for its own sake. This intrinsic quality of experience can be an object of desire in its own right; it is necessary (over time) for any other intentional object to be sustained as an object of desire; and it is the key to the intrinsic satisfactoriness of an experience, whether that experience was an object of prior desire or not.

There is thus truth in the ancient view that we desire x because it is good; x is not good because we desire it. It has often been supposed that this view requires an objective theory of intrinsic value that could not be made part of a naturalistic theory. What RET can claim is that intrinsically positive hedonic tone both fulfills that ancient formula and plays a clear, empirically supported role in the natural psychology of many creatures.

There is another criticism of RET that a good naturalist could make, however. RET admits that the Reward Event mechanism no doubt evolved to keep creatures focused on and willing to work for external goals such as food, water, and sex, that are essential for biological flourishing and reproduction. This is the biological point of the mechanism, and in that sense what it is "supposed" to do.[8] If, for a naturalist, the real objects of perception are the biologically appropriate external objects (rather than a brain event), why should that not also be true of motivation or desire?

The argument has force. A partial reply is to note the differences between perception and motivation. While one can induce visual experiences by direct stimulation of the brain, it has seemed easy to say that in these cases we only *seem* to see something. But no psychologist or neurologist has ever said that when a creature is working away to produce Reward Events in the brain, it only *seems* to be motivated to produce such events. The independence, and potential dominance, of Reward Events as objects of motivation cannot be ignored.

Finally, it should be noted that, as throughout this book, I have sketched only a half theory. In addition to a theory of positive value, a theory of negative value is also needed. Unsurprisingly, for RET, negative value is negative affect or hedonic tone; this tone is seen as intrinsically negative and as playing a contingent role in the shaping of behavior. Once again, that role is to be determined empirically. Thus, a complete theory would postulate not only Reward Events, but also Aversion Events. The corresponding neuropsychological theory would provide evidence for such events that could be triggered directly in the brain. There is a large body of evidence dealing with pain (as a key example of negative affect), and the evidence is complex, but I will simply be assuming that there are Aversion Events, which play a role analogous to (though usually opposite from) that of Reward Events. Briefly, the real punishments would be internal, affective, and only contingently connected with other states of affairs.

Let us now note the philosophical commitments of RET. The theory is realist—some events do have the properties of being intrinsically good (positive) or intrinsically bad (negative). These properties are intrinsic properties of these events. Because this is so, the theory is also externalist (in the sense mentioned above in the discussion of Mackie), that is, the intrinsically good is not conceptually connected to (defined in terms of) any relation to motivation or desire (or, for that matter, cognition). The connections between Reward (or Aversion) Events and desire and action are contingent, causal connections. The intrinsically good (or bad) is a property of subjective psychological states, but it is not in any other sense subjective or relative. It is an objective truth—true for all—that there are states with intrinsic, positive (or negative) value.

Does the theory meet the naturalistic constraint? The answer to this question depends ultimately on how the empirical evidence develops, but this situation is true of any theory operating within some naturalistic constraints. To date, the theory is at least consistent with a considerable body of empirical evidence. Admittedly, support for RET requires a certain conceptualization of that evidence, but I have argued that this conceptualization has theoretical virtues and may be most empirically fruitful.

What of the plausibility constraint? If the empirical evidence is at all reliable, then for RET, the intrinsically good (positive affect or pleasure) does in fact play a major role in causing motivation and action, not only in human beings but also in many other creatures. Indeed, should the strongest form of the neuropsychological theory turn out to be correct—that Reward (or Aversion) Events are both sufficient and necessary for the sustaining of desire and action over time—then it could be claimed that only RET meets the plausibility constraint. Any rival theory that would claim that there is intrinsic value (or disvalue) in events or states other than those subjective psychological states that are Reward (Aversion) Events would be claiming that something has intrinsic value that in fact is never desired for its own sake, is never that which is the real cause of motivation and action, and that may be realized in experience without that experience being at all satisfactory.

It should be clear by now that some of the issues raised by RET are empirical issues, and for resolving these we have to wait on developing scientific theories. But other issues are more conceptual or philosophical—or are at least in the foggy interface between science and philosophy. Two issues are central: (1) Does it make sense (or the best theoretical sense) to think of pleasure as an intrinsic quality— a quality of positive hedonic tone—rather than as a relational property defined in terms of motivation or desire (a question we began discussing in the previous chapter)? (2) What is it for a property to be a value property? Has RET really made a case that positive affect is a value property—is intrinsically good? What happened to the normative? These are proper questions; I will deal with them in the context of comparing RET with alternative theories.

PLEASURE: INTRINSIC OR RELATIONAL?

In dealing with the above questions, the taxonomy of relational theories has to be complicated even further to indicate important divisions within the class of conative-relational theories.

One version could agree that pleasure is an intrinsic quality but insist that pleasure is a purely descriptive, nonvalue property. It is the intrinsically good (positive value), the theory could say, that is to be defined in terms of a conative-relational property. Thus, pleasure may or may not be good, or may be good in some contexts and not in others. In addition, many other things may well be intrinsically good. Let us call this the ID (Intrinsic/Descriptive) view of pleasure.

A second version could say that pleasure is indeed a descriptive, nonvalue property, but that it is a relational property of experiences, defined, for example, in terms of one's being motivated to (or desiring to) prolong the experience, where no constraints are put on motivation. Constraints are instead introduced in the definition of intrinsic value. And once again, no assumption is made that pleasure as such is good. Let us call this the RD (Relational/Descriptive) view of pleasure.

Finally, a third version could hold that pleasure is indeed a value phenomenon—for an experience to be pleasant is for it to be intrinsically good—and that both the pleasantness and the value of the experience are to be defined in terms of appropriately constrained desire or motivation. Let us call this the RV (Relational/Value) view of pleasure.

In terms of this taxonomy, RET is an IV (Intrinsic/Value) view, that is, pleasure is an intrinsic property of certain psychological states, and pleasure as such is good—has intrinsic value, where this value is an intrinsic property of those states.

RET is at odds with all three of the above views (ID, RD, and RV) on whether value (intrinsic goodness) is an intrinsic or a relational property. For all three, value is relational; this issue will be dealt with in the next section. In this section, I continue the previous discussions of how to conceptualize pleasure.

This debate is complex; appeal has been made to everything from introspection of one's own phenomenal experience to scientific fruitfulness in psychological theory. My strategy has been to point out difficulties for the alternative theories and advantages for RET.

RET and ID (the Intrinsic/Descriptive view of pleasure) agree that pleasure is an intrinsic quality. Where they do not agree is on whether pleasure as such is good, but this disagreement is primarily about value and will be dealt with in the next section.

Consider, next, the RV (Relational/Value) theory, in which pleasure is defined in terms of suitably constrained motivational states, constraints that constitute pleasure as a value—as good. The first thing to be noticed is that if the constraints are constraints on the motivational states of the subject of the pleasure, and if those constraints involve a considerable degree of reflection—or rationality—then it could turn out that no nonhuman animals ever experience pleasure (or pain).

The most important disagreements about pleasure, conceptually and empirically, are between RET and RD (the Relational/Descriptive view). Leaving aside issues of value, RD claims that we should conceptualize pleasure (and correspondingly pain) in terms of certain motivational states. A sophisticated form of such a theory, one which draws heavily on psychological theory and is thus very much in the naturalistic spirit of RET, is the theory developed by Brandt (1979). Brandt offers the following definition:

'the experience E of the person P is pleasant for P at t': [=df] 'an experience of the kind E is going on in the person P at t; and the experience E is the differential cause at t of an increment in the positive valence of the continuation of E beyond t . . .' (40)

Add to this the earlier definition Brandt gives for 'valence':

a person 'wants' something O, or that something O 'is valenced for' him at the time, if his central motive state is such that if it were then to occur to him that a certain act of his then would tend to bring O about, his tendency to perform that act would be increased. (26)

Brandt also notes that "there are other tendencies which are lawfully related to valence, indicative of it, and partially define its meaning" (26), tendencies having to do with disappointment, elation, dispositions to think of certain events, and so forth. (And of course there are parallel definitions of aversions or negative valences.) Brandt summarizes his view of pleasure: "In short an experience is pleasant if and only if it makes its continuation more wanted" (p. 40).

Brandt is very skeptical about there being any common intrinsic quality of all those experiences (legitimately?) called pleasant. However, he does concede that those theories (such as RET) that assert that the intrinsic quality is not any localized sensation, but is rather a pervading hedonic tone, are the most plausible. Nevertheless, he finds such a quality "elusive" (38) and has even stated (in private correspondence) that "I can't identify any such thing in my experience." He also believes there are theoretical advantages to his "theoretical construct" definition of pleasure. What can RET say in reply?

Debates about what one can or cannot find in introspection often seem fruitless, even if one does not assume that each person has, through introspection, full and totally accurate knowledge of all intrinsic qualities of his or her own experience. Nevertheless, some things can be said. First, as RET would emphasize, hedonic affect is usually not the conscious focus of experience. That is most often directed to external states of affairs, or (in introspection) to intentional content or to specific sensory qualities. There are, however, many reports in the psychological literature of subjects describing experiences in terms of pleasurableness or hedonic quality, as a report of what the experience is like. Of particular note are reports of certain drug experiences, in which the dominant characteristic is intense euphoria, sometimes to the exclusion of any other experiential content.[9] Psychologists willing to work with introspective reports have generally taken reports of hedonic quality as reasonably accurate descriptions of a common aspect of experiences otherwise quite different in content. This evidence is not conclusive, but it does provide support for the claim that positive hedonic tone is the relevant intrinsic quality of experiences of pleasure.

Brandt does not, however, rest his case solely on introspective appeals. His primary aim is to argue for the theoretical advantages of defining pleasure as a "theoretical construct defined by its relation to behaviour" (36).

Since Brandt's definition is operational in form, most practicing psychologists would officially endorse this kind of definition, particularly if they wish the concept of pleasure to function in theories applicable not only to humans but also to nonhuman animals who cannot give introspective reports. This would seem to be a real advantage for any naturalistic theory and would thus favor Brandt's version (or some version) of a DR (Descriptive/Relational) theory over RET.

In reply, as noted above, in practice many psychologists do accept introspective descriptions of hedonic tone, and only get methodological qualms if they have to apply those descriptions to the experiences of nonhuman animals. Such analogical extensions may seem altogether too speculative, particularly when contrasted with the purity of treating all subjects as behavioral black boxes. But behaviorism and operational definitions are no longer assumed to be the only possible methodologies, nor does Brandt make any such assumption.

Let me note again a theoretical disadvantage of defining pleasure in terms of motivations and related actions; this parallels the arguments given in chapters 2 and 3 for the disadvantages of defining reward operationally, in terms of the shaping of behavior. If pleasure is defined in terms of positive motivations (or reward in terms of such shaping), then one cannot appeal to pleasure as an independent explanation for such motivation (or for such behavioral effects). If, as in Brandt's definition, "an experience is pleasant if and only if it makes its continuation more wanted," then one cannot say that the continuation of the experience is more wanted because it is pleasant, if that "because" is to be a causal explanation. Even as a conceptual claim, this would be misleadingly backwards; one ought to say that the experience is pleasant *because* its continuation is more wanted. Pleasure could not play an independent explanatory role; explanation would be entirely in terms of conative (and cognitive) states. By contrast, RET claims that a psychological theory that recognizes an independent causal role for positive (and negative) affect or hedonic tone can provide concepts and explanations that best fit the growing neuropsychological evidence about the role of Reward Events in the brain.[10]

Motivational (or other relational-property) theories of pleasure have tended to concentrate on focused experiences of pleasure, experiences with specific sensory and/or intentional content. According to these theories, such sensory or intentional content does not as such constitute a pleasant experience; such content is pleasant only if it stands in the appropriate relation to, for example, certain motivational states. Whether the experience does have the required relational properties is a contingent and changeable fact.

The rival account given by RET is that such focused experiences, if they are experiences of pleasure, contain both sensory/intentional content and an intrinsic quality of positive hedonic tone, and that these two aspects of the experience are only contingently connected. The further claim is that any motivational effect of the experience is due to the hedonic tone, not to the other contents, though these contents do have an informational role in focusing and steering the motivation (e.g., in terms of seeking further experiences with that content, as sources of pleasure).

Since RET has an extra property in its explanations, parsimony might seem to favor some relational-property view. But this presumed advantage is less obvious when one considers unfocused experiences of pure pleasure. Such an experience, as in some reports of unfocused euphoria, would be entirely affective and would have no other sensory or intentional content. According to RET, the experience would be constituted by an instance of positive hedonic tone. While such an experience might be motivating, in the sense of causing a desire for more experiences of that kind, the experience itself would contain nothing that could focus or steer that motivation. If the experience just happened, and not through any controlling action of the one having the experience (e.g., it is not seen as the result of drug ingestion, or a course of meditation, or the like), then one might just hope for the return of such an epiphany. This seems a plausible characterization of these experiences. By contrast, theories that define pleasure in terms of some motivational phenomena directed toward some other aspect of experience have no place for experiences of pure pleasure, and this lack is a disadvantage of these theories.

RET would give comparable accounts of negative experiences. The theory would caution against labeling these experiences as pain, since the paradigm pain experiences are experiences with specific sensory content. According to RET, the sensory content plays an informational role (e.g., in steering motivation), but what makes the experience negative, a bad experience, is the presence of the intrinsic quality of negative hedonic tone, a quality that can exist in the absence of any sensory or intentional content and that constitutes experiences of pure awfulness.

Up to a point, this account agrees with those (see Nelkin 1986) who have argued for a distinction between pain and pain sensations. Any theory needs to account for the fact that certain kinds of surgery or anesthetics can produce experiences that are paradoxically reported as "painful but it doesn't hurt," or "painful but I don't care."

Apart from the label issue (should these "nonhurtful" experiences be called pain), the key theoretical issue is whether the missing hurtfulness or badness is constituted by a *reaction toward* the sensory content (as was defended by Nelkin 1986; he has recently modified his view to make the missing ingredient an "evaluation" of the phenomenal state [1994]) or is instead constituted by an intrinsic quality of negative hedonic tone that contingently causes such reactions, as RET would claim. And once again, while parsimony might seem to favor a relational-property view, RET's intrinsic property view gives a better account of pure awfulness.[11]

There may be, far in the future, more directly relevant neurological evidence. The empirical bet of RET is that developing theory will distinguish three distinct types of brain circuitry—that necessary for producing sensory or intentional (informational) content, that necessary for producing affect (intrinsically positive or negative hedonic tone), and that necessary for producing motivation or any tendencies to action. If we are then able to produce experimentally, through control of brain circuitry, three such distinct states that are only contingently connected, this result would be confirmation for RET.

RET, or any theory making pleasure and pain (broadly conceived as positive or negative hedonic tone) intrinsic properties, will leave it an open, empirical question how these properties are related to motivation—or to any intentional or sensory content. As I have argued, this position makes narrow psychological hedonism (hedonism with respect to which kinds of psychological states creatures are motivated to pursue) an empirically testable causal claim, as it surely should be.

RET also allows for the empirical possibility that some creatures in fact are motivated to pursue pain and/or avoid pleasure. Of course, these should be unusual exceptions, if RET is to meet the plausibility constraint on value.

It should be clear by now that both an intrinsic-property theory of pleasure (as in RET) and a relational-property theory (such as Brandt's) have their advantages and disadvantages. What these are may change with developments in scientific theory. If a neuropsychological theory that gives a central role to Reward Events (and aversion events) continues to be fruitful, and if my conceptualization of such a theory is plausible, then I think there are good reasons to accept an intrinsic-property theory.

The case will be strengthened if such a theory also gives rise to a plausible theory of value. Here, however, suspicions may return. Perhaps it can make sense to define pleasure as an intrinsic property, so that there is only a contingent connection between pleasure and positive motivation (or pain and negative motivation), but can this contingency make sense for good and bad—for positive and negative intrinsic value? Can there be only a contingent connection between the good and positive motivation, without getting into such metaphysical extravagances as Forms of the Good or nonnatural properties? Furthermore, how does value get into the picture? We must now turn to the disagreements between RET and relational-property theories of value.

VALUE, THE NORMATIVE, AND IDEOLOGY

According to RET, intrinsic goodness is an intrinsic property of certain experiences—experiences had not only by humans but by many nonhuman animals. If evolution had veered so that we never appeared, but there were solitary creatures with experiences of pleasure, there would be intrinsic goodness in that world, even though (by hypothesis) these creatures never reflected on their lives, never faced social pressures to behave one way rather than another, and never knew or were influenced by any norms. Their actions would be caused, but not guided.[12] (Parallel claims could be made about intrinsic badness and pain.)

A counterclaim could be that the function of value is to *direct* choice and to provide a basis for *criticizing* any particular choice, preference, or liking. Value is a matter of *standards* and *evaluations*. Values are norms that somehow guide action.

As a preliminary reply, it can be noted that if RET is correct, the key causal grounding of motivation is in Reward Events, which usually are not the objects of focus. As already noted, the "because" of RET is not the "because" of conscious practical reasoning. Since standards and evaluation do have their roles in such reasoning, by focusing on a deliberative perspective, we may miss the key phenomena.

It should also be noted that direction, evaluation, and criticism are often interpreted so as to require considerable cognitive sophistication. If value is confined to these contexts, we may have to restrict intrinsic value to the lives of the cognitively sophisticated. The range of affect (which is central to RET) is wider than the range of sophisticated deliberation ("How shall I lead my life?").

Nevertheless, with respect to our own lives, explicit evaluation has no doubt done much to shape our thoughts about intrinsic value. In addition to the potential ambiguities of ground and focus, inherent in our psychological mechanisms, there are competing conceptions concerning the function of value, constituting competing ideologies of value.

To dramatize the issues raised by the function of intrinsic value, I will tell two, admittedly extreme, stories. Each story emphasizes a different aspect of our motivational mechanisms, and each postulates a different function for value.

The first story could be called the Outwardly-Focused-Keep-Them-Working story, but that is a bit awkward, so let us call it simply the Whole-Life story. Remember that the Reward Event mechanism no doubt evolved because it kept creatures focused on and motivated to work for those external objects needed for biological success. Add, now, to this external focus the conviction that value, as a director of choice, should help us to make it through a life. How plausible, from this perspective, that value should attach to fairly stable external goals. And if it is seen (for sundry social, political, and economic reasons) as of utmost importance that we keep pursuing certain goals, even if direct reinforcement fails altogether, then there might be even stronger insistence that the value is out there, in the goal itself; if motivation falters, the goal has not failed, we have. This is value as externally located and socially stabilizing.

The second story could be called the Inwardly-Focused-Timeless-Delight story or perhaps the Haunting Epiphanies story. Now there comes to the fore, not merely the essential causal role played by Reward Events, but particularly their ability to be the direct (indeed, the only intrinsically direct) objects of motivation. Initially, it might seem odd, based on the laboratory evidence, to contrast this story with a Keep-Them-Working story, since the rats work steadily for their ESB, bar pressing to the point of collapse. I would argue, however, that this frantic activity is also an artifact of the laboratory, and that the rat would be perfectly content, thank you, to have the ESB zapped in with no effort on his part.[13] No achievement motive here. The Reward Event itself, while it is going on, does not motivate a creature to do anything; it simply brings about joyous acceptance.[14] It is only when the world, with cruel indifference or malicious intent, snatches away the Reward Event that activity is induced. While the Reward Event is present, there need be no concern for, perhaps no sense of, any passing of time.[15]

Value is now attached to experiences, mostly stripped of any outward focus, that do not motivate one to do anything but rather bring other activity to a halt in a kind of timeless acceptance. We might say that such value has finality. It is not novel to ascribe such a characteristic to the highest value; if one has the highest, why move on? Furthermore, in contrast to such experiences, all standard goals might be seen as pale or totally inadequate substitutes, and if the world were such that these epiphanies were rare, one might be haunted by their absence.

It could be troubling if such experiences tended to undercut all other goals and motivations, though this might be less troubling in a culture more accepting of mysticism than ours or more comfortable with a quietist stance toward life. Nevertheless, there is the potential for such value, against the backdrop of "normal" social structures and economies, to be very destabilizing or even radically subversive. The Timeless Delight view could even see it as the function of value to recall us from the world of false external goals.[16] This is value as internally located and (potentially) socially destabilizing.

I shall have to return to these broader issues of ideology in the next chapter, when I deal with the implications of RET for a theory of the good life. What I think is already clear is that the normative is likely to be highly contextual, social, and related to competing *human* practices. We should not assume that the same is true of the intrinsically good; that is, we should not assume that the good is normative. From a naturalistic perspective, I think we have good reasons for identifying the intrinsically good with an intrinsically positive quality of experience that is good in its own right, independent of any wider context, including the nature of the creature having the experience.

This view is further reinforced by the clarity of the (postulated) central causal role played by Reward Events, which are not only sufficient for a highly rewarding experience but are also (if RET is correct) necessary for any other kind of experience or activity to be rewarding and motivating. Not only should a theory of intrinsic value be prior to and independent of the ethical, it should also be independent of the normative in all its forms.

Such independence from the normative is particularly critical if one wishes to develop a realist theory of value that can fit into an overall naturalistic picture. If one ties intrinsic value to the normative, one will tend to make totally obscure, at just the key points, how such intrinsic value can play a causal role in motivation. I will have more to say about these issues in chapter 6.

NONNORMATIVE VALUE

The normative has to do with reason giving, justifications, practices, and a host of other social, contextual, cultural, historical, and ideological factors. Whether one can find anything objective in that tangled web is a complicated issue and should not call in question intrinsic value as an objective intrinsic property of certain subjective, phenomenal psychological states. Like the rain, intrinsic value appears in the lives of the just and the unjust, the human and (in many cases) the nonhuman.

The value and disvalue of positive and negative hedonic tone are real properties of those psychological states. And such value can plausibly play a straightforward role in our psychology and in the psychology of many other creatures. What the neuropsychological evidence suggests is that affective states play an independent causal role *as affective states*, rather than only a secondary role, through cognition of (beliefs about) such affect or desire for such affect. The propositional attitudes do not exhaust our psychology; in focusing primarily on such content-bearing states (as in belief/desire models), one is leaving out what are likely to be the only phenomena through which objective, intrinsic value entered the world and can be part of a natural, causal picture.

In what sense, then, are positive and negative affect—positive or negative hedonic tone—values? It is right there on the face of it. Positive hedonic tone *is positive* and in that sense is *good*. Negative hedonic tone *is negative* and in that sense is *bad*. These intrinsic properties of hedonic experiences *are* their value—no more and no less.

Such a bald assertion will not, at this stage of the argument, be persuasive. Any adequate theory of value must defend the implications of the theory for two central questions:

1. What does the theory have to say about what constitutes a good life? Can any theory that confines intrinsic value to qualities of conscious experience reply adequately to the many criticisms of such mental-state theories? These questions provide the topics of the next chapter.

2. How is value related to norms—to those characteristically human practices of giving reasons for actions, of judging actions as right or wrong, of setting moral standards? One of the naturalistic truths about humans is that we are social creatures, and a theory of value must help to make sense of these complex social practices. The challenge is to make value sufficiently independent of these practices so that it can be acknowledged that there is intrinsic value in the lives of many nonhuman creatures, while not making value so independent that it becomes irrelevant to these further, normative questions. This issue will be the topic of chapter 6.

5

Summing Up the Good Life

I have argued that positive hedonic tone is intrinsically good—(probably) the only natural property that is intrinsically good. Hedonic tone is a quality within conscious experiences, and thus all intrinsic value is *within* sentient lives.

What, then, does RET tell us about what constitutes a good life? For many, this is *the* big question, not only for philosophers but for any reflective being, and is of more than theoretical interest. We have distinctively human capacities to be reflective and self-reflective, to engage in second-order assessments of our experiences, beliefs, preferences, choices, actions, and even of our lives as a whole. Such capacities are central to many people's understanding of value and the good life.

We need, however, to interpret the question, What constitutes the good life? and even this first step will be controversial. I will interpret the question as asking: What makes a life intrinsically good *for the creature whose life it is*? In other words, I am bracketing the impact of that life on other lives except as that impact makes a difference to the original life. I am thus in large measure bracketing any moral assessment of that life. This procedure may seem question-begging, particularly for those who would see our moral qualities as at least partially constitutive of a good life.

My preliminary reply is to note that one legitimate focus is on the intrinsic value of a life, as opposed to any instrumental value it may have with respect to other lives. Whether that brackets moral qualities depends, of course, on one's theory of intrinsic value as well as on one's theory of morality. If one believes that intrinsic value can be realized by states of affairs that are not within any conscious experience, then there is indeed room for the intrinsic value of a life to be constituted by all sorts of relational properties—social, moral, and otherwise.

By contrast, any theory confining intrinsic value to aspects of conscious experience must see the intrinsic value of a whole life as somehow a summation of the intrinsic value of stretches of experience. Such a locus of value has seemed to many to be obviously counterintuitive and to be inconsistent with what we really want for our lives; this appeal to intuition is seen as a strong argument against any such theory of intrinsic value. If a theory cannot make sense of the good life, then it certainly cannot be the whole story of intrinsic value.

In reply, I will use the psychological theory of RET to explain, though not to justify, these counterintuitions. I will defend the positive view that the intrinsic value of a life (for the creature whose life it is) is indeed constituted by a summation of positive hedonic tone,[1] and that this hedonic tone is only contingently connected with all those other aspects of experience on which creatures are usually focused. It will turn out that in one sense all good lives (human or nonhuman) are the same, while in another sense they are enormously varied, both within and across species.

MAXIMIZING

If only positive affect has positive intrinsic value, then any intrinsic value in a life must be constituted by instances of such affect. This aspect of conscious experience is sometimes present and sometimes not. The least contested dimension of such experiences of affect is thus temporal dimension, though even here problems can be raised based on the presumed differences between clock time and experienced time. If, as the common report goes, pleasant stretches of experience seem to go by much faster than do unpleasant stretches, and if experienced time is the relevant measure, then the ironic result would be that the more pleasant experiences we had, the less total intrinsic value we would have. Euphoric experiences reported as timeless would constitute the vanishing point of value! Such paradoxes strongly suggest we had better stay with clock time as the relevant measure of the temporal dimension. It follows that, other things being equal, if life A has a greater total duration of positive affect than life B, then life A has the greater amount of intrinsic value and thereby is the better life.

Once we go beyond temporal dimensions, the measurement questions become more difficult. Are there differences in intensity of positive affect, and if so, what kind of scale does this establish? Different answers have different theoretical implications for the ranking of lives. For example, Mendola (1990) has argued for a purely ordinal ranking: experiences can be ranked as more or less positive (or negative), but we can give no meaning to the relative size of value differences (such as that the difference between A and B is greater than the difference between B and C).

Are rankings of pleasure and pain purely ordinal in the way Mendola claims? There are counterintuitions: Surely the difference between screaming agony and a dull ache is greater than the difference between the ache and a minor twinge. There is also evidence from psychology, in which subjects are asked to rank experiences hedonically or to make other rankings of intrinsic qualities of experience.

Introspection is, of course, often very fallible. Any adequate theory of the mental will include properties and processes that are not accessible to introspection at all. Other properties may be possible objects of introspection, but in so far as these are complex relational properties (e.g., beliefs), there is likely to be a good deal of interpretation and commonsense theorizing involved in introspective reports. All introspective reports may be to varying degrees theory-laden, but if the report is of an intrinsic quality of present conscious experience there should be the potential for a reasonably accurate report, including reports of the intensity of hedonic tone. (Duration can be externally clocked.)

Might there be other dimensions of pleasure (and pain), however, that are relevant to its value, beyond its intensity and duration? Specifically, what of the presumed distinction between quantitative and qualitative hedonism? The classic historical source for the distinction is Mill (1861), who argued that pleasures can differ not only with respect to duration and intensity (quantitatively) but also with respect to kind. Such a theory has been severely (and I think justifiably) criticized, but it has recently been revived and defended by Edwards (1979).

As discussed in chapter 2, Edwards develops a relational-property theory of pleasure—"the generic meaning of 'pleasure' is 'the set of all feelings we desire or wish to sustain or cultivate'" (95)—and goes on further to specify such "desire" by saying that pleasure means "the set of all feelings for which we have a psychic tension or attraction" (95). As Edwards then points out, and as is true of any relational-property theory, such desires or wishes can be focused on—have as their objects—a wide variety of different feelings or contents of experience (including, Edwards makes clear, much intentional content). What he concludes is that pleasures thereby differ not only with regard to any quantitative dimensions but also qualitatively in terms of these various intentional objects. He sees these qualitative differences (in the spirit of Mill) as providing a basis for ranking pleasures not only in terms of intensity and duration but also in terms of kind. (This ranking is to be accomplished, again much like Mill, in terms of the preferences of the majority of "qualified judges" who meet various criteria of judgment and "rationality" and who have experienced the various pleasures to be ranked.)

Apart from this theory being a relational-property theory of value, is this a hedonism, much less a qualitative hedonism? The key is Edwards's claim:

> Intentional pleasures and pains may be distinguished from one another by their objects, that is, those nonaffective properties of experience from which they are *inseparable* [my emphasis]. Intentional pleasures and pains are like specific desires, which are always desires *for* something, and which can be distinguished from one another only as we specify what they are desires for. (87-88)

Consider some intentional content, such as engaging in philosophical activity. This content (an experience of engaging in such activity) is not as such a kind of pleasure. We must "desire or wish to sustain or cultivate" that experience before it can be an instance of pleasure, and such reactions to that activity are in no clear sense inseparable from that activity. It is quite possible (and no doubt actual) that a person at one time will have that reaction to such activity and at another time will not. This is also true with respect to any other intentional content. On Edwards's own theory, what constitutes any experience as a pleasure for S is that S "desires or wishes to sustain or cultivate" that experience. This is the pleasure-making property, a relational property that can, indeed, be true of a wide variety of objects but is by no means inseparable from such objects.

This conclusion is not changed if one interprets Edwards as claiming that pleasures are essentially "*feelings* for which we have a psychic tension or attraction [my emphasis]," and that such feelings are an additional element of the experience beyond any intentional content. Thus, for example, the experience of engaging in philosophical activity would be constituted by both distinctive intentional content (e.g., thinking about Hume's theory) plus a kind of feeling that is phenomenally distinctive of that content. The feeling that goes with philosophical activity (or perhaps more specifically with thinking about Hume) would be different in kind from, say, the feeling that goes with listening to music (or specifically to Beethoven) or drinking wine. Even with this complication of Edwards's theory, however, no such feeling is as such a pleasure; if one has such an experience with its distinctive feeling but does not have a "psychic tension or attraction" to the feeling, it will not count as an instance of pleasure. Once again, it is the desire or wish to sustain the experience that is the pleasure-making property. And it is the pleasure-making property that must supply any dimensions of pleasure as pleasure; on a relational-property view, the dimensions will be the intensity and duration of the desires and wishes, which is as purely quantitative as any other hedonism.

If, in the preference ranking of the values of various kinds of pleasure, the ranking is the same as the ranking in terms of the pleasure-constituting desires and wishes, then the theory is indeed hedonism, but it is quantitative hedonism. If, on the other hand, the ranking departs from the rankings in terms of intensity and duration of the desires and wishes, perhaps by placing special constraints on whose desires and wishes count, then the theory is perhaps not quantitative (though presumably it is still the intensity and duration of these qualified desires that counts), but it is also not hedonism. It is no longer the pleasure-making properties of the experiences that are the basis for their value. Nor will it be hedonism if the value ranking is done on the basis of the kind of intentional content and/or feeling distinctive of such content. Since neither of these aspects of the experience constitutes it as an experience of pleasure, such value is not hedonistic.

The distinction between a theory, such as RET, that makes the value property an intrinsic quality of experience and a theory that makes the value-constituting property some relational property of other contents of experience can be used to counter Moore's claim (1913) that "hedonists have always meant by pleasure the consciousness of pleasure, though they have not been at pains to say so . . . ," and that this thesis is incompatible with hedonism because, if true, "pleasure is not the *sole* good" (90).

First, it is not at all clear that consciousness and pleasure are two distinguishable and separable aspects of experience, as if there could be unexperienced pleasures. Some contemporary theorists who distinguish different kinds of consciousness might defend such a view, but it is doubtful that Moore would. As discussed in chapter 3, I am inclined to say that pleasure is an intrinsic quality of conscious phenomenal experience and is the quality that makes such an experience good.

Suppose, however, that the consciousness is a separable property, say some relational property of an experience with the intrinsic quality of pleasure. Is Moore saying that the consciousness is, in its own right, a value-making property? But then the consciousness of pain would make the experience of pain at least a partially good experience, one better than an unconscious pain; the consciousness of an otherwise neutral intrinsic quality such as a buzzy tone would make that experience intrinsically good. No sane hedonism need accept these results.

There is in Edwards the suggestion of a different theory of the nature and qualitative differences of pleasure. This theory is worth discussing in its own right; it comes closer to making pleasures intrinsic qualities of experience, independent of any wish to sustain and repeat them. As Edwards puts it:

> If pleasures and pains differ qualitatively, then there are different species of pleasure and pain, just as there are different species of color and figure. We never directly experience pure pleasure or pure pain as such, just as we never directly experience pure color or pure size or shape. We do experience particular instances or species of color, such as red or blue, and particular species of shape, such as circles and triangles. (86)

The color analogy is suggestive and is perhaps better discussed in terms of a *determinable* and its *determinants,* since "species" suggests the possibility that all the instances possess certain qualities in common that make them members of the same genus—a view that Edwards rejects (see p.35).

The theory (not explicitly developed in Edwards) says that pleasure is a determinable and that all we actually experience are determinants of that determinable, such as pleasure-of-contemplation, or pleasure-of-Chablis, or pleasure-of-winning-the-lottery. We should not be misled by the appearance of the word 'pleasure' in each of these labels; in principle we could coin distinct terms for each kind of experience, just as we have the terms 'red,' 'blue,' and 'green.'

What, then, constitutes each of these experiences as a pleasure experience? (Compare: What makes instances of red and green and blue all instances of color?) If this theory is not to collapse into a relational-property theory, the reply cannot be in terms of any attitudes or responses toward the experiences nor in terms of any common causes, effects, circumstances, and so forth. (That reply would be analogous to: What makes an experience a color experience is that it has its source in some appropriate complex of physical stimuli and brain circuits.) Instead, the theory must say that there is some introspectively obvious relation among all the experiences that makes it clear that they are all pleasurable (or, analogously, are all color experiences).

As a presumed description of our pleasure experiences, I find this theory less perspicuous than RET's description—that all the experiences, while differing widely in *associated* content, share a common quality of positive hedonic tone. Thus, one can have an experience of contemplation, or of tasting Chablis, or of winning the lottery that is exactly the same in terms of intrinsic qualities or content as the comparable pleasure experience except that it lacks the intrinsic quality of pleasure, a quality that can be experienced in isolation.

When Edwards does discuss those "species" of pleasure and pain that do not involve intentional objects, he says, "If there are such objectless pleasures, they cannot be identified and distinguished by reference to objects, as can intentional pleasures. . . . Objectless pleasures and pains have to be distinguished conceptually from one another either in terms of their causes or sources. . . ." (87). These relational properties do not, of course, constitute the experience as a pleasure (or as a pain). The greater puzzle is what constitutes it as an experience. There is no intentional content, and Edwards seems to rule out a distinct nonhedonic phenomenal quality (of the kind suggested in my previous discussion of the role of feeling in Edwards), since otherwise we would not have to resort to causes or sources to distinguish these experiences. He also rules out any distinct hedonic quality. There seems little left that one could "wish to sustain."

Setting aside these difficulties, let us pursue the color analogy and consider the implications for a qualitative hedonism. The theory could say that every instance of intrinsic value is an instance of a pleasure experience. The differences in value of these experiences do not, however, consist only of the differences in their intensity and duration. Instead, or in addition, some kinds of pleasure rank higher in value than other kinds. The differences in kind are determined by either differences in intentional object, or by differences in causes or sources, or (to stay closer to the color analogy) by differences in nonhedonic phenomenal quality. (Compare: All value experiences are color experiences, but their values do not differ solely in terms of such quantitative dimensions as degree of saturation, but also in terms of their determinate colors. Thus, an experience of blue is a better experience than an experience of red of an equal degree of saturation just because it is that kind of color. We might call this "qualitative colorism.")

This theory might work out as a qualitative hedonism if the differences in value are determined by the differences in the kind of experience and *if* the different kinds of experience are all pleasures just because, in some intuitively obvious way, they fit together. (Compare: Unless we can make a clear case for why red and blue are both colors and for why all value experiences are color experiences, the theory might not be colorism but, say, bluism. It might just be an accident that the determinate experiences that have value are all color experiences.)

If, instead—and as is closer to Edwards's theory—the different kinds of experiences are all pleasures because we desire to sustain them, and we desire to sustain (or prefer, or what have you) some kinds of experiences more than other kinds, and the differences in degree of value are determined by the differences in degree of desire, then the theory is quantitative hedonism.

If, however, the differences in degrees of value are determined by differences in the kinds of experience, independent of their status as pleasures, then the theory is not hedonism. I am inclined to conclude that unless someone can come up with a persuasive version of a determinable-determinant hedonism (hedonism as colorism), any viable hedonism is going to be quantitative.

RET claims that positive and negative hedonic tone are intrinsic qualities of experience, which can be ranked by intensity, even if this ranking does not establish full cardinality. Thus, there can be a summing up of the intrinsic value realized within a life, based on intensity and on duration. While this estimate is bound to be at best rough, it may not be realistic to expect any greater precision, particularly if value is a suitably naturalized property.

PREFERENCE AND MAXIMIZING

It is often assumed by many economists and social scientists that qualities of conscious experience (e.g., pleasure and pain) are hopelessly subjective and that any properly objective and scientific study of welfare must be based on preference as manifested in choice. Many contemporary utilitarian theories are forms of preference utilitarianism, rather than the more traditional mental-state utilitarianism.

If one recognizes, however, that choice and preference are very complex psychological phenomena, and that interpreting these objective data involves many theoretical assumptions, it may no longer be so obvious that preference theories have an advantage over mental-state theories. Indeed, few preference theories are based on raw preference; most require that preferences be rectified before they can serve as a measure of welfare, a rectification involving further theoretical assumptions (see Gauthier 1986).

There are, in addition, special problems for preference theories of value in specifying what is to count as *maximizing* such value. The general point has been forcefully made by Brandt (1979) in his discussion of what he calls the "desire theory," which "identifies welfare with desire-satisfactions" (247). Even if such a theory puts restrictions on the desires whose satisfaction is to count (e.g., that they be reflective, considered, or that they have survived what Brandt calls "cognitive psychotherapy"), the concept of maximizing the satisfaction of desires is, Brandt claims, "unintelligible" (249). "The problem for the desire-satisfaction theory arises," he argues, "from two facts: first, that occurrent desires at a time t are for something to occur (to have occurred) at some other time; and second, that desires change over time" (250).[2]

As an example of the problem, consider a person who has had for thirty years a very strong and reflective desire that she retire to a place on the Oregon coast. Then, a few months before the time of retirement, due to various personal and circumstantial changes, she now has an equally strong desire to retire to a place in the Sonoran desert. If a benefactor could, at the time of her retirement, give her a place either on the Oregon coast or in the Sonoran desert, which gift would contribute more to maximizing the satisfaction of her desires over an entire lifetime? There may be various ad hoc solutions to such problems, but the suspicion is that they are covertly based on the consideration—which events the person will actually find satisfactory when they come to pass. Such an appeal to experienced satisfaction comes much closer to making the value of the event contingent on experienced quality (on positive affect, according to RET), rather than on its being contingent simply on the coming into existence of the intentional object of a desire.

As Brandt recognizes, it takes a certain "temerity" (251) to argue against preference theories, since they dominate in contemporary rational-choice theories, which have defined various sophisticated and technically elegant conceptions of maximization. But when a philosopher, such as Gauthier (1986), builds on such theories to develop a theory of value, the problems recur. Gauthier presents one such problem: "It is not rational, the defender of prudence claims, simply to maximize the fulfillment of one's present preferences, however considered they may be, if one does not take into account the preferences one will or may come to have" (36). Gauthier's reply, for a number of good technical reasons, is that "practical reason takes its standpoint in the present" (38). And it is from that standpoint that Gauthier develops his theory of value as utility, as a measure of considered preference.

Consider again our problem case. Suppose the benefactor has to purchase the gift land ten years prior to the recipient's retirement. By hypothesis, at the time of the purchase, the recipient still strongly desires to retire to the Oregon coast. Suppose that the benefactor knows that the person's desires will change, and that by the time of retirement, she will strongly prefer retiring to the Sonoran desert. What should he do to maximize the satisfaction of her preferences? What reason is there, within the bounds of the satisfaction-of-desire theory of welfare, to give greater weight to her future preference over her present, long-standing preference?

Indeed, suppose our retiree herself knows that her desires will change in this way? What Gauthier says, consistently, is that unless she has a present preference for satisfying her future preferences (37-38), she has no reason now to purchase land in the Sonoran desert, rather than on the Oregon coast. Maximization must be based on present preferences. But any value maximized in this way would seem to be only contingently related to the lived quality of experiences, and thus, from the perspective of RET, only contingently related to the intrinsic value of a life for the person whose life it is.

A further problem arises within the technical development of Gauthier's theory. Gauthier rejects any appeal to qualities of experience, or enjoyment, or hedonic tone as the basis for value (35-36). Thus, value must be grounded in the satisfaction of preference as such, that is, in the coming into existence of a preferred state of affairs. Now consider Gauthier's discussion of the transitivity of preferences, one of the formal conditions required for maximization as defined in rational-choice theory:

> Suppose that Bruce has an apple. Before he eats it we offer him a peach; he prefers the peach and so he trades. Before he eats the peach we offer him a pear; he prefers the pear and so he trades. But before he eats the pear we offer him the original apple; he prefers the apple and so trades. After three trades, in each of which Bruce betters his situation in terms of his preferences, he finds himself at his starting-point.
>
> Indeed, Bruce's situation is even worse than this example suggests. If he prefers a peach to an apple, then presumably he is willing to offer more than the apple in return for the peach. Suppose he is willing to offer 1¢. And suppose he is willing to offer the peach and 1¢ for the pear, and the pear and 1¢ for the apple. Then after three trades, in each of which Bruce betters his situation in terms of his preferences, Bruce finds himself with his original apple but 3¢ poorer. . . . And clearly Bruce, who becomes *ever less well off* [my emphasis] as a result of trades, each of which betters his position in terms of his preferences, is engaged in an irrational sequence of preferences. (41)

But by what standard of value are we to measure Bruce's welfare, before and after his trades? Consider first the pure trade sequence, with no money involved. At the end, is Bruce "at his starting point"? By no means; he now has in his biography three more satisfied preferences. At the time of each trade, he got what he preferred, which is by no means to find himself "at his starting point." By what conception of value, according to Gauthier, has he made no progress?

There may be a clue in the second case, which brings in money, and in the fact that the rational-choice theory on which Gauthier draws is central to much economic theory. In this case, we are presumably to see Bruce at the end not only back where he started from but 3¢ *poorer*. He is, Gauthier says, "ever less *well off* [my emphasis] as a result of trades." But unless Bruce has a preference for money for its own sake, why is he less well off? Why shouldn't he use his cash to satisfy his present preferences? It cost him 3¢ to have, at the end, three more satisfied preferences in his biography, but we expect to have to pay to satisfy many of our preferences.

The moral of such examples is, I believe, the very one Brandt drew (1979, 251-52). Even if, in the technical literature, there are intelligible programs of maximization (of whatever it is the theory specifies is to be maximized), how convincing are they if we are supposed to see that which is maximized as the intrinsic value that is central to a creature's having a good life? While initially plausible, when looked at more closely, preference theories seem less and less persuasive.

Thus, with respect to the measurement problem, we should not assume that all the advantages are with preference theories. The extensive psychological literature suggests that measurement grounded in intrinsic qualities of experience can be as reliable as that grounded in preference (taken as the basic phenomenon, rather than as an indirect measure of felt satisfaction or dissatisfaction). If there can be reasonably accurate rankings of positive (and negative) hedonic tone, these rankings can then be combined with duration to provide a very rough overall summing up of affect within a single life— and one no rougher than that provided by any other plausible measure of those properties of a life that make it a good life for the creature.

Beyond this issue of an overall summing up of intrinsic value, there is a further issue based on an implicit assumption (at least as old as Plato) that if we know what has intrinsic value (the Good), this knowledge will tell us how to lead our lives. If not strict rules, one hopes at least for usable guidelines.

No matter what its specific theory of measurement and ranking, the high-level rule of any hedonism will be: The best life is the life with the best balance sheet. Indeed, this is the rule for any view that makes the overall value of a life a resultant of the intrinsic value and disvalue of distinguishable stretches of conscious experience.

In the face of the unhelpful nature of such a rule, what further can be said by RET? The central point is this: The connections between intrinsic value (positive affect) or intrinsic disvalue (negative affect) and any other contents of experience are contingent, and it is thus an empirical question which activities and experiences produce such affect, to what degree, for how long, and with what side effects. We learn about these connections from individual experience, from observation of others, from history, from literature, and even from philosophy. Evidence and advice from the past will be of varying relevance in new circumstances and can at best be probabilistic. There is no basis for saying, with a priori confidence, that *this* way of life *must* be a life of intrinsic value, or that *that* way of life *cannot* be a life of intrinsic value. We should be prepared to be surprised at the forms of life from which people receive positive affect, and at the forms that make them miserable.

No doubt sensible things can be said, and some of them have even been said by those ostensibly criticizing hedonism. The often-cited "paradox of hedonism" could be interpreted as telling us that the best way to achieve the best balance sheet of affect is not to aim directly at this result but rather to focus on nonhedonic goals. This claim may sometimes be true. And postponing gratification can be a useful strategy, though scarcely a rule for a whole life.

There are challenging technicalities about balance sheets; but for many critics, neither technical elegance nor internal coherence will be convincing, in the face of strong intuitions and arguments against any hedonic theory of intrinsic value, or even any mental-state theory that limits intrinsic value to qualities of conscious experience. I will now consider some of these counterintuitions; my aim will be to explain them psychologically, and to do so in a way that will defuse their force as evidence against my version of a hedonic theory of value.

RETROSPECTION, ANTICIPATION, AND OVERVIEWS

The more technical and precise one makes a theory about the drawing up of a balance sheet of hedonic affect for a whole life, the less this theory will seem to have anything to do with how people actually sum up their lives at different times. By "summing up," people generally mean assessing a life's overall value. From this overview perspective, they usually do not see the value as constituted by a net sum of hedonic affect; their focus is on all sorts of other properties. What can RET say about these counterintuitions derived from reflection?

While it is doubtful that we are the only creatures who remember past events and anticipate future events, what may be distinctive is the characteristic human activity of periodically looking back on our lives *as our lives*, or of anticipating or planning some future as *our* future. Such overview reflection involves a special kind of intentional content. It nevertheless shares with less reflective types of content the possibility of becoming associated with positive (or negative) affect and thereby entering into our motivational structure. Such associations can lead to some curious results. Two results can be illustrated by two examples—one from real life and the other from literature.

From real life, there is the fascinating autobiography written by A. B. Facey (1981) at the age of 83. Born in 1894 in the Australian outback, Facey lost his father before he was two, and his mother deserted him soon thereafter. He went out to work, under a savagely sadistic master, at the age of eight. He went through the Gallipoli landing in World War I and lost a son in World War II, commenting, "My experience in the First World War and now the Second World War changed my outlook on things. It is hard to believe that there is a God" (317). There were the years of struggle through the Depression of the 1930s and a series of different occupations, plagued variously by drought, labor unrest, and so on. And, yet, Facey titles his book, without a trace of irony, *A Fortunate Life*.

The literary example is from Milan Kundera's *The Unbearable Lightness of Being* (1985), a novel in which the characters tend to display the hyper-reflectivity of the modern temper. At one point in the novel, Tomas and his wife Tereza are living in Switzerland, having fled the Czechoslovakia of 1968. One day Tomas finds a letter for him from Tereza, telling him she is leaving him and returning to Prague, that "she was weighing him down and would do so no longer" (28). Here are Tomas' reflections following this event:

> He was depressed, but as he ate, his original desperation waned, lost its strength, and soon all that was left was melancholy. Looking back on the years he had spent with her, he came to feel their story could have had no better ending. . . .
>
> He paid the bill, left the restaurant, and started walking through the streets, his melancholy growing more and more beautiful. He had spent seven years of life with Tereza, and now he realized that those years were more attractive in retrospect than when he was living them.
>
> His love for Tereza was beautiful, but it was also tiring. . . . Now what was tiring had disappeared and only the beauty remained. (29-30)

This is just one of Tomas' reflective episodes, as he examines and reexamines his relationship with Tereza (which is resumed). And each new overview brings a different summing up.

One lesson of these examples, of course, is that the externals of a life often tell us little or nothing about the quality of that life for the person living it. This is a direct implication of RET, which stresses the contingent, variable, and often surprising connections between specific experiences and positive or negative affect.

The point I would make is more complicated, however, and centers on the claim that an overview of a life is a separate experience, with its own affective qualities, that may bear little relationship to the net sum of the affective qualities of the past experiences being surveyed or of future experiences being anticipated.

A. B. Facey's summing up was a 326-page book, the creation of which, one senses, was itself a very satisfactory experience. The book ends with these lines: "I have lived a very good life, it has been very rich and full. I have been very fortunate and *I am thrilled by it when I look back*" (326, my emphasis). With Kundera's Tomas, there is an endless series of summings up, and summings up of summings up, with no one reflective episode portrayed as any more authoritative than any of the others.

We are thus faced with potential discrepancies between the actual affective qualities of a stretch of life and the affective qualities generated by reflection on that life. The phenomenon is not confined to surveys of a whole life but can occur any time one reflects on a past experience or anticipates a future one.

Such discrepancies cannot occur in nonreflective creatures. With them, motivation is more closely tied to the contingencies of reward and aversion generated by first-order experiences. These contingencies are not a completely reliable guide to the future—circumstances can and do change—but there is a kind of natural prudence to a life so closely attuned to actuality. And if we take an overview of such a nonreflective life in order to judge whether it was a good life for the creature, it seems altogether reasonable to judge on the basis of the net sum of affect, as best as we can determine such qualities.

This claim is not completely uncontroversial, even with respect to nonreflective lives. Some have seemed to argue that for wild creatures a free life is a better life than life in a zoo, even if the latter contains significantly less suffering and significantly more pleasure (see Rachels 1989). I say "seemed" because it is no doubt true that in the history of zoos, many wild creatures have not flourished in captivity. But if they do? There is something attractive about claiming a Kantian dignity for the lives of wild creatures, but I suspect we are being influenced by the positive affect of our overview of their lives in the wild, and it is not at all clear that this anthropomorphic perspective should carry weight. In brief, not only are nonreflective creatures[3] natural maximizers, at least in stable contexts where past affect is a reasonable guide to the future, but a net-sum view of what constitutes a good life for them seems most sensible.

The issue, then, is whether the ability to reflect makes a difference with respect to what constitutes a good life. If this were merely a matter of there being a new kind of content to which affect can attach, there would be nothing distinctively new. Presumably, each species capable of affect has its own distinctive kind of nonaffective content—delights of the nose for the dog, delights of the ear for a bat, and so on. Indeed, there are likely significant differences within species, though we tend to overlook these in our useful biological generalizations. So, the fact that we can gain positive (or negative) affect from reflection on past experience, from anticipation of future experience, from stories we tell ourselves about our own lives, or from imagination, fantasy, and so on, simply adds to the great variety of content that can become contingently connected with affect.

We can, so to speak, enjoy an experience many times over—once in the living of it—and an indefinite number of times in anticipation and memory. More darkly, we can receive negative affect many times over. It is not really accurate, however, to say that different instances of positive (negative) affect attach to the same experience. Anticipation, or memory, or any overview experience is its own distinctive kind of experience, just as much as deliberate fantasy or imagination. So why not just add these new instances of affect to the balance sheet in considering the overall goodness of a life?

If the affect attaching to an overview experience, prospective or retrospective, mirrored with reasonable precision the affective qualities of the experiences that are the objects of reflection, then the only problem might be a suspicion—analogous to the "double counting" problem in utilitarianism[4]—that some kinds of experiences were gaining disproportionate influence on our motivation through being more often mirrored in reflection. But the problem seems minor. If certain kinds of experiences, for whatever reasons, are particularly effective in producing the pleasures of anticipation and memory, we could welcome such fecundity.

The assumption of accurate mirroring is, however, clearly contrary to fact. There are, of course, many instances of accurate mirroring, but there are as many, if not more, instances of discrepancies between the affect of an experience and the affect of reflection upon that experience. There are the distortions of memory, the delusions of anticipation, the softening effects of time, and the changes in us that lead us to look back with pleasure on experiences by no means pleasurable or to look back with aversion on what we once enjoyed. There can even be a kind of simultaneous double vision, as in the would-be saint, filled with horror at his own current sexual pleasure. Above all, what patching, filling, omission, and downright invention go into those stories we tell ourselves about our own lives. How important it is, to so many of us, to find a pattern in our lives (some would call it a meaning), though the pattern is often only in the telling.

If one considers these many different kinds of discrepancies between the affect of a first-order experience and the affect of a reflection upon that experience, or between the balance sheet of affect in a whole life and the affect of an overview of that life, it is by no means obvious that value is best understood or realized from a reflective perspective. Such a perspective does indeed constitute a different experience, and one which is in a semantic sense second-order, but just as the later in evolution is not thereby higher,[5] so a second-order experience is not thereby higher or better.

If there is no privileged standpoint from which to assess a life, in the sense that the affect produced by reflection from that standpoint determines the value of the whole life, we are left with a balance sheet in which the positive or negative affects of reflective overviews are simply added to the balance sheet as one more possible kind of content. I think this conclusion is right, but I need to explain further why it may not seem right.

According to RET, positive affect is the only intrinsic motivator and the only intrinsic positive value; but any understanding of specific motives and of the details of a life must pay attention to focus—to those intentional contents that, through reinforcement by positive affect, may become directly motivating, as opposed to being pursued only as a means. These are the goals that people will often cite as those that they are pursuing for their own sake. Insofar as this claim involves a belief in the functional autonomy of such goals, it is, according to RET, a mistaken belief. Nevertheless, these outwardly directed goals play a major role in explaining the details of a life. In any individual case, it is an empirical question as to whether the affects of a reflective overview outweigh, in terms of effective motivation, the affects of the experiences reflected on.

And is it obvious which should win? Consider our would-be saint. If horror wins out over sexual desire, is this a triumph of the soul or one more instance of the distortion of human life by "monkish virtues"? Some (including our would-be saint) may take an overview of this contest itself (thus taking a third-order overview) and may view the triumph of horror with positive affect, while others may find such an outcome deeply aversive. These affects, of course, have no more authority than those of the second order or the first order.

Suppose now—as may occur in some cases—a particular conception of the good life has gained sufficient reinforcing affect to become a dominant motivator for the person holding that conception, that is, in the main, her life is directed in ways that roughly fulfill that vision of the good life. Suppose, in addition, that fulfilling this vision requires undergoing many first-order aversive experiences, perhaps more than if her conception had simply been to maximize pleasure. If, as we are assuming, these first-order negative affects are dominated by the positive affect of her overview experiences, we have the result of someone whose motivation is indeed causally grounded in positive and negative affect, but who would probably deny that she is a maximizer. If this is a genuine possibility, it is so only for one capable of a reflective overview of her own life.

The key point is that reflection on actual or possible experiences or even on a whole life may, contingently, generate positive affect. If this happens, the reflective experience is thereby a source of intrinsic value. It does not follow that the experiences that are the objects of the reflection are sources of a corresponding intrinsic value. If, for example, a past experience was one of negative affect, and thus one of intrinsic disvalue, no later reflection on that experience that sees it in a new light and that generates present positive affect can transform that past experience into one of intrinsic value. (One could, of course, see it as having been causally necessary for a later intrinsic value.) The intrinsic value or disvalue of an experience is an intrinsic property of that experience, and the intrinsic properties of a temporally specified stretch of experience do not change over time.

This is a major difference between RET and those naturalistic theories that make intrinsic value a relational property of experiences, such as being the object of a reflective preference. Relational properties of a temporally specified stretch of experience can change over time, and as noted, it is a major problem for preference theories to deal with such changes. If I now prefer A to B, and later prefer B to A, which preference should count? This eventuality poses no theoretical problem for RET. For RET, there are no privileged times of life, or perspectives, or reflective overviews that dominate in constituting intrinsic value. The theory can acknowledge that reflection may contribute to a practical wisdom about which experiences do in fact generate intrinsic value, though such wisdom is equally likely to be a result of nonreflective learning on which we are not explicitly focused. The theory can also explain why, for reflective creatures, there can be so much distortion and mythology about the intrinsic value of individual experiences or even of whole ways of life.

One such way of life is life in the notorious Experience Machine. This is the philosopher's favorite sci-fi machine; it can generate for an individual plugged into the machine a complete and consistent illusion that one is leading a real life, and this illusion can generate a strongly positive balance sheet of affect. Such a machine is, of course, just a technical updating of Descartes's Demon.

This thought experiment has generated in many philosophers strong intuitions that they are convinced discredit any theory confining intrinsic value to intrinsic qualities of conscious experience. Griffin, for example, says, "we do seem to desire things other than states of mind, even independently of the states of mind they produce. This is the point that Robert Nozick has forcefully made with some science fiction [the Experience Machine]. . . ." (1986, 9). Similarly, Brink says, "Value cannot consist in psychological states alone. Robert Nozick's experience machine explains why. . . . Each of us wants to *be* a certain kind of person and *do* certain sorts of things and not merely have experiences *as if* he were such a person doing such things. . . ." (1989, 223-24).

Theorists such as Brink do, of course, accept the possibility of individual experiences in the Experience Machine having intrinsic value or disvalue. To deny this possibility would lead to the implausible conclusion that no one in an Experience Machine ever suffers in a way that counts as an intrinsically bad experience or ever has any intrinsically good experiences.

The claim being made by Brink, Nozick, and others is that value cannot consist in psychological states alone, and that a life with nonexperiential values, such as real accomplishment, is (necessarily?) better than one with only good experiences. It is not sufficient for these critics to say that nonexperiential values are different kinds of value that, if present, can add to the overall value of a life. If that were all they were claiming, the implication would be that an Experience-Machine life could be a good life, though one lacking in some particular kinds of value. Such a lack would be comparable to the lack in a good life of some kinds of (or sources of) experienced value; given the temporal limitation of human life, any life will lack some kinds of value. The critics must claim that nonexperiential values somehow trump experiential values or necessarily rank higher than any experiential values, so that even a life with a preponderance of intrinsically good experiences cannot be a better life than a life with some nonexperiential values.

If nonexperiential values (doing certain things or being a certain kind of person) necessarily rank higher than any experienced values, the implication would seem to be that a life of genuine accomplishment but of unrelieved suffering (lacking even any sense of satisfaction with one's accomplishments) is necessarily a better life than an Experience-Machine life of constant joy. There are those who might accept this conclusion, but I find such fierce austerity totally implausible. The only plausible locus for the intrinsic value that makes a life a good life for the individual living that life is within experience. RET then makes the further claim that within experience, only the intrinsically positive (or negative) hedonic qualities have intrinsic value (or disvalue). All other contents of experience are possible sources of, or can be associated with, these values but are intrinsically neutral.

Intuitions generated by the Experience Machine typically arise from an appeal to what we really want, or desire, or prefer, and thus beg the question in favor of a preference theory of intrinsic value. As already noted, relational-property theories have major problems in dealing with changes in desires or preferences over time. For example, suppose that a person is in the Experience Machine and knows that she is in it, and while undergoing the fantasy experiences strongly prefers staying in the machine to returning to real life. Even if, while out of the machine, she prefers being out, why should this second preference count over the preference in the machine? Should the preferences of youth count over the preferences of old age or vice-versa? If a person has a radical change of personality, beliefs, and so on, should the prechange preferences or the postchange preferences be the ones that constitute the value in the overall summing up of the life?

One may also question whether preferences should be considered ultimate with respect to explanation. Consider a preference for A over B, where A and B are two different kinds of experience. How are such preferences formed, and more to the point, how do such preferences become "informed" in the way generally required by those theories that make preference a measure of intrinsic value? Surely being informed must involve actually experiencing A and B. Is it, then, that after such experience we just find, as an ultimate phenomenon, that we now prefer A to B? It is, I believe, more plausible that there is an explanation for such preferences grounded in the intrinsic qualities of A and B, specifically in their intrinsic hedonic qualities.

Furthermore, change of preference needs a comparable explanation. Suppose someone prefers A to B, a preference created by past experiences of A and B. If this person later comes to prefer B to A, it is plausible to postulate that there has been some change in the person such that, for example, experiences of A no longer generate as much positive hedonic tone as do experiences of B.

In addition to such explanation, it also seems most plausible to ground the value of the experiences in their actual experienced quality, rather than in the preferences generated by that quality. Indeed, even so-called preference theories of value have recognized that it is not preference as such that is the key, but rather the *satisfaction* of preference. If preference is understood as a motivational phenomenon, then it is not the wanting of A or the desiring of A that produces value; it is the having of A. And at that point the familiar phenomenon looms—that often people want A very much and are strongly motivated to pursue A, but on obtaining A, do not find it at all satisfactory. Thus it is not satisfaction of desire or preference in the minimal sense of getting what one wanted that is the key to value; it is the felt satisfaction—the actual hedonic quality of the experience—that makes it one of intrinsic value.

As for preferences for states of affairs that are not qualities realized within conscious experience (which preferences have been used to criticize any mental-state theory of intrinsic value and of the good life), they lead to their own paradoxes. Can it really be the case that the coming into existence of a state of affairs after the death of a person (e.g., posthumous fame) can really make a difference to the value of that life for that person?

Even if the state of affairs occurs during the lifetime of the person (as, for example, in real achievement as opposed to the faux achievement of illusion, deception, or the Experience Machine), if the difference between such a reality and its simulation never makes any difference to the intrinsic qualities of conscious experience, it is not plausible to suppose that the difference constitutes a difference in the intrinsic value of the life for that person.

The point gains force if one wishes to defend a thoroughly naturalistic theory. A naturalized theory of intrinsic value needs to show how intrinsic value is a natural property and how this value property can play a role in the psychology of living creatures. Even if a naturalistic theory of value is grounded in relational, nonqualitative properties such as belief and desire, the function of these properties in psychological explanation does not depend on the truth of the beliefs or the realism of the desires. Thus, if intrinsic value depended on such nonexperiential dimensions of belief and desire as their truth or realism, the value would play no explanatory role.

By contrast, mental-state theories in general, and hedonic-quality theories in particular, can explain both the psychological role of intrinsic value and how it makes a relevant difference to the lives of creatures. Naturalized intrinsic value has its most plausible locus within conscious experience; and within conscious experience it should be seen as consummatory, as being good in its own right, and thus as an intrinsic quality of experience.

Intrinsic value, as an intrinsic quality of conscious experience, is independent of any wider context; thus RET, unlike preference-based theories, need not select a single context as the correct one for specifying value. Given the problems such selection has generated for preference-based theories, this result is a further advantage for RET or any intrinsic property theory.

To further explain the counterintuitions used to criticize mental-state theories, RET says that the preferences generated by the affect attaching to an overview of an Experience-Machine life as compared to the overview of a real life can be very misleading about the intrinsic values realized within those two lives, and that this is no different in principle from the way we are often misled about past or future experiences within our real life. Memory can distort, and we often desire at one time that something be the case at a later time, and when we later get what we wanted, the experience is not at all positive and thus does not add to the intrinsic value of our life.

RET can also appeal to the possibility that in the future there will be fairly strong empirical evidence. If we can come to control in the brain the presence or absence of positive affect in ways that leave unchanged any other contents of experience, then it might be shown that the presence of positive affect is both intrinsically positive and generates motivation directed to any associated content, while the absence of affect eliminates the perceived value of any other content of experience (including true beliefs about what we have accomplished and so on) and, over time, extinguishes any positive motivation directed toward such nonaffective contents.[6]

No one of these arguments is conclusive, but together they suggest that we should not take at face value intuitions generated by reflection and overviews or by Experience-Machine thought experiments; such intuitions can mislead, and RET has an explanation for why they are likely to do so.

SELF-IMAGES

At this stage, a critic might claim that RET is missing the central point: that value has to do with evaluating, with passing judgments on experiences, actions, and lives, with assessing reasons for or against candidates for value. We are distinctively rational beings, and surely this rationality must be at the core of any theory of value or of the good life.

This criticism focuses a key empirical issue. RET claims that only positive affect is intrinsically good; it also claims that only affect (positive or negative) is intrinsically motivating—motivating in its own right. No cognitive content—judgment, reflection, the giving of reasons—is intrinsically motivating, and so cognitive content, in line with our plausibility constraint, is unlikely to be the key to intrinsic value. Cognition may, of course, become directly motivating, through the contingencies of association with affect, but this possibility is true of any content that may become the focus of motivation.

For RET, these claims primarily apply to our judgments about intrinsic value—about our ends. While not as central to the theory, the claims may also apply to that paradigmatic, and least controversial, example of our practical rationality—means-end rationality. Belief that, or even knowledge that, a particular course of action will produce pleasure or prevent pain may not be able, on its own, to motivate that action. (Remember Damasio's cases of the failure of "practical reason.") Cognition, or perhaps more likely an imaginative anticipation, may need to carry appropriate affective associations. Prudence is not a universal motivation, nor is the failure to be prudent necessarily a cognitive failure.

RET hypothesizes that judgments—be they of prudence, morality, or of the specifics of a good life—do not motivate by virtue of their cognitive content but by virtue of their affective associations. Consider the implications of this claim for self-reflection.

Most people's conception of a good life includes not just doing certain kinds of things but also being a certain kind of person. Such conceptions are consistent with almost all modern psychological theories of motivation, which stress the key role of one's self-concept or self-image. Such a role for a self-concept is consistent with RET, which can readily accept that this distinctive type of content has strong affective associations and thus plays a central motivational role.

Indeed, this central role for a self-image is altogether to be expected in a social creature capable of self-reflection. If we assume a motivational role for one's self-image, we can explain additional intuitions that have led philosophers to reject any hedonic or affect-based theory of value.

"Suppose," a critic might say, "it could be established with high probability that you would have a far higher net sum of positive affect in your life if you were to change radically (perhaps through that all-purpose philosophical tool, brain surgery), so that in the future your frequent and intense positive affect would be generated by your new-found fundamentalist religious beliefs, along with long daily sessions in front of daytime television, regular attendance at stock car races, and participation in Texas rattlesnake roundups, in which you will be very effective at bashing rattlesnakes. Now, would you accept such changes? And if not, is that not inconsistent with your own theory of value?"

First, in reply to the question as to whether I would accept such changes, the answer is, of course, no. My refusal is certainly not inconsistent with RET. Nothing in the theory commits one to the view that the only content that can be directly motivating is a belief that one's choice or action will produce the greatest possible net sum of positive affect. Affect can only play its causal role in motivation in association with some intentional content, but it is not the thought of affect that plays that causal role. We do not "do" affect, we do various things that generate affect, and we do them because similar actions in the past have generated affect or because the thought of such an action has become associated with affect. The association may be due to the actions being seen as the actions of a specific kind of person and to seeing oneself as that kind of person having gained its own affect. Thus, my refusal to accept the proposed new life of greater positive affect is unquestionably due in part to the very negative affect I attach to the thought of being such a person, an affect that easily dominates any affect attaching to the relatively abstract thought of maximizing positive affect, even though that thought has the interest of being stated in terms of my own theory.

What, then, of value? First, it does follow from RET that each episode of positive affect in the proposed life of a religious rattlesnake basher would indeed be an instance of positive intrinsic value. And it may be true, by hypothesis, that such a life would have more net positive value than will my own (unchanged) life. But the thought of this increase in positive value, embedded in the thought of its being the life of that kind of person, is, for *me*, strongly negative. At the same time, it is also true that if I were to change in this radical way, I would have a good life in two senses—I would have a highly positive net sum of affect in my life, and my reflections on that life—my thought that I was that kind of person—would also be strongly positive. I am not so changed, however, and thus my thought (mostly abstract and theoretical) that such a very different life would be a good life in the senses indicated carries nothing like the affective charge of my negative overview of that life. And any motivationally effective overview must be taken from one's own actual psychology. In terms of motivating content—the focus of motivation—very few of us may be maximizers in the sense of being directed by a conception of the good life that involves only a concern for the greatest net sum of positive affect. At the same time, our actual motivations (assuming the correctness of RET's theory of motivation), including our motivating conceptions of a good life, are causally dependent on positive and negative affect, the only intrinsic motivators. And no matter what the nonaffective content of our motivations and lives, these affective events provide the only instances of intrinsic value and disvalue.

ALIEN LIVES

Suppose that one knows that a life has contained a strongly positive net sum of affect. Suppose, in addition, that the nonaffective content of that life—the kinds of experiences found pleasurable, the sorts of goals pursued—is quite radically different from one's own. How are we to judge whether that is a good life?

Start with those other lives of other species. Such lives have often been seen as alien in the minimal sense of being far different, perhaps unimaginably different, from our own. In addition, in much of human history they also have been seen as alien in a more pejorative sense. They are brutish lives, with all that claim has connoted.

In part, this negative overview may result from a curious comparison of their lives with our lives. The comparison is curious ·because it suggests that we are to choose between living our own kind of lives and living their kind, and thus that I am to decide whether this sloth had a good life by deciding whether it would have been a good life for me. And that conjecture is in turn deeply ambiguous, between imagining myself leading the sloth's life as a sloth, which is probably incoherent, and imagining myself doing sloth-like things, which would probably not give *me* the same balance sheet of affect.[7]

If one avoids such confusions, and if one has developed a reasonably Darwinian sensibility, it is quite possible, not only to acknowledge that positive affect can attach to very different kinds of content, but also to take a very positive overview of this biological variety. How splendid that there should be so many curious kinds of lives![8]

We should be careful here about what we are acknowledging. In the first place, there is the recognition that we share with many forms of life a psychology of affect, and that we thereby have the same capacities for realizing intrinsic value in our lives. This recognition does not anthropomorphize other species, nor does it zoomorphize us. It is a recognition that intrinsic value is not species bound. And this implication of RET I find particularly welcome.

At the same time, we are acknowledging that due both to wired-in genetic differences and to differences in the learning contingencies of any individual life, the particularities of that life—the experiences found pleasurable or aversive, the goals pursued—can be enormously various.

For many post-Darwinians, this is not a threatening conclusion with respect to other species. To put the point rhetorically: Why shouldn't a sloth have a good life? And why should we have ever supposed it would have to be our kind of life? Indeed, why should we suppose that all sloths have the same kind of good life?

And yet, the conclusion seems curiously more threatening—at least to many—when brought closer to home and applied to the enormous variety of human lives. Perhaps this fact is not surprising; the foibles of family members are usually more embarrassing than those of strangers. More accurately, we may sense that acknowledging that a sloth has a good life does not commit us to saying that it would be a good life for us. It is a kind of life that is not even a possibility for us. When we consider other human lives, however, we do see them as possibilities, and we want to reject some of those possibilities. How are we to assess this reaction? Consider two very different kinds of cases.

Consider first a human life in which there is positive and negative affect generated by the satisfying or the failure to satisfy basic biological needs, but in which those are the only conditions that can generate such affect, since there is almost no cognitive development—in other words, a condition of extreme retardation. Can that be a good life? If there is a reasonable balance of positive over negative affect, there seems no more reason to deny its being a good life than to deny such a possibility to the life of a sloth.

But is it a good life for a human being? Well, given this particular human being, with those particular capacities, it is a good life for her. Just as different sloths may have different kinds of good lives (with respect to nonaffective content), so may humans.

Does this acknowledgment commit me to saying that it would be a good life for me? The question is now more complicated. What am I to contemplate? Is it that I, this psychologically complex being who is the object of my self-reflection, am that sort of person? This is of course incoherent, as incoherent as imagining myself as a sloth. The question can cut closer to home, however, if we take a more bodily based view of personal identity. Couldn't I become that sort of person, in a way that I could not become a sloth? And could I see that change as just entering another kind of good life, rather different from my present life?

With such a radical psychological change, and in particular with the loss of any reflection or self-reflection, I am still inclined to say that it would not be me. More circumspectly, this would be a kind of psychological death. So what I am contemplating is replacing my psychological life with another, far different psychological life. Both lives may be good lives, but the only life with which *I* can identify is the life that has an "I" that reflects and self-reflects. How can I contemplate that other life as a good life for me when I can't even contemplate it as me?

Next consider cases all of which involve the capacity for reflection and self-reflection. My life and the life of the religious snake-basher are just two examples from the enormous variety of human lives.

Let me first enter a caveat, raised by that snake-bashing component of a life. Such a component raises ethical issues that I am bracketing. I wish to consider whether a life is a good life for the being living that life and leave it as a separate question whether the life has any morally questionable impact on other lives. If we are assessing the lives of other species, the separation is straightforward; they can have good lives, but it is doubtful that moral assessment of their lives is applicable. (This may depend on one's theory of the psychological conditions necessary for moral responsibility and on an adequate theory of the psychologies of other species.)

With humans of normal capacities, the separation is more controversial. RET does not allow that being a moral person is intrinsically good, though it can agree that for many people, seeing themselves as moral carries strongly positive affect. It is also true that it can make a great difference to other lives which sorts of contents—of reflection and self-reflection—become associated with which sorts of affect. For now, however, the ethical dimension will enter only as an aspect of a self-image, of being a particular kind of person.

Now, let us suppose that I have one sort of life and see myself as one sort of person and that the fundamentalist has a very different sort of life and a very different self-image. Let us also suppose that each of us reacts with positive affect to the thought of leading her own sort of life and being her own sort of person, while reacting with strongly negative affect to the thought of being that other sort of person leading that other sort of life. Does either of us have a basis for saying that the other is not living a good life?

We are now at the heart of the matter. If all those other sorts of species can have good lives, why not all sorts of humans? Does the mere fact that they are all biologically human put any constraints on what can be a good life for them?

RET can accommodate some constraints; which constraints would be an empirical question. Which sorts of experiences and activities and which sorts of self-images are capable of being associated with positive affect in humans? Perhaps no human could ever find sitting on an egg the rewarding experience it probably is for many birds. But many of our activities would no doubt be as opaque to them. So our biology and our psychological mechanisms make a difference.

There may be, for example, the possibility of making an empirical case for the greater value of cognitively complex lives. One could speculate—and at this stage of research it is sheer speculation—on a kind of affective connectionism. Suppose an experience has, through past experiences and/or through exercise of the imagination, become cognitively associated—that is, associated through nonaffective content—with a large number of other kinds of experiences, concepts, beliefs, and so on, up to and perhaps even including a world view. The experience sets off a whole neural network. Suppose also that not only does the experience directly connect with positive affect, but also that the associated neural network, both through separate circuits and perhaps through some global action, triggers additional positive affect in a way that magnifies the overall positive affect, sustains it over time, and makes it more resistant to extinction and more effective in long-term motivation. This result would give empirical grounding, within RET, for that sense we often have of the special significance of experiences funded by past experiences and by wide cognitive associations. Cognitive complexity would still not be intrinsically positive, but it could have a significant causal role. Of course, such networks could also magnify negative affect, so there would not be pure gain. For RET, whether complexity of cognitive content increases the positive value within a life is an empirical question.

Empirical constraints like these are not, however, the sort of constraints philosophers have usually had in mind. The thought has been that reflection on the many different kinds of lives of which humans are biologically and psychologically capable can provide a basis for judging that only some of those lives are good lives, even if all are filled with positive affect.

As I have argued, however, reflection on a kind of life is just one more kind of experience. It does not even provide a privileged standpoint for assessing our own lives, much less for assessing the lives of others.

But wait. Have I not been doing just that? Have I not been pronouncing lives to be good on the basis of their affective content? In a sense this is true. If instances of positive affect are the only events with positive intrinsic value, then it follows (trivially) that every instance of positive value in a life is an instance of positive affect. This tells us nothing, however, about the other contents of that life or about any overall shape or pattern to the life.

As mentioned earlier, knowing what is the good cannot tell us how to lead our lives. Discovering what provides positive value is much more a matter of trial and error or deliberate experimentation. We have also discovered that reflecting on our lives as being certain kinds of lives and on our selves as being certain kinds of selves can also be strongly affective and can sometimes be a dominant motivation. But just as, at the first-order level, different people find different sorts of activities rewarding, so at the reflective level, different people find different visions of a kind of life or of a kind of self rewarding. The connections between positive affect and any other contents are contingent connections, and nature is lavish in her experiments. Perhaps the post-Darwinian stance would be to see each individual human being as his or her own species.

It is this naturalistic perspective I would stress in response to lingering counterintuitions. "Can you really mean," a critic might say, "that a life wired in to a minimalist Experience Machine that provides all and only pleasure with no other content is a good life for a human being? Is that not so obviously absurd as to constitute a reductio of your theory?"

First, note again that what I mean by a good life for the individual is a life with a preponderance of good experiences; I do not mean a life with some presumed nonexperiential holistic value. According to RET, the relevant nonmoral intrinsic value is a natural quality within experience.

Next, consider another case a critic might raise and which might seem even more challenging than the example of life in a minimalist Experience Machine. Using whatever moral theory you find persuasive, imagine a person who is totally vicious, as morally bad as possible. Now the question is, Can this vicious person have a (nonmorally) good life?

RET's answer is, Yes, this is of course a possibility. Rather than being yet another reductio of the theory, this answer is a straightforward implication of seeing intrinsic value as a natural property with only contingent connections with other properties or events or states of affairs. The good enters lives both through the actions of individuals and through the accidents of nature. Good experiences are not distributed by some cosmic, justice-oriented force.

A parallel question makes the point more poignantly. Can good people, morally splendid people, have a preponderance of bad experiences? Again, the answer is yes, and again this is an expected result of good and bad being natural properties of experiences. Even those with a religious perspective that allows for a cosmic justice-dispensing force find it difficult to answer this question with a no.

If, then, even the morally vicious can have a preponderance of good experiences, it should not be surprising that an individual in the minimalist Experience Machine could also have this sort of good life.

A critic at this point must insist that to have a good life is for the life to have some kind of value that is independent of the experienced quality of the life for the individual. RET rejects there being any such extraexperiential value; the rejection is not obviously absurd.

To return from sci-fi fantasy to realism, given the complex neural interconnections in the human brain, and given interesting laboratory results (Porrino 1987) that suggest that even in the rat brain the reward circuits are only activated through self-stimulation (the rat's own activity) rather than through experimenter-administered stimulation, there may be an empirical case for a life of activity and variety being the most reliable source of the good. If this turns out to be the case, then we will have established a contingent truth about human neuropsychology, not an a priori truth about the good.

LIFE UNDER THE FORM OF CONTINGENCY

It has been the hope of many philosophers, and the conviction of many nonphilosophers, that it can be shown that what we care about has intrinsic value (and what *they* care about does not).

Perhaps it has been assumed that if we could make such a case, we would have provided a special sort of protection for the things we care about, which are often so very vulnerable. With greater realism, we have recognized that destruction can always take place, and that philosophical argument is a frail defense against force. Still, there could be some philosophical consolation in being able to say that what is taking over is barbarism.

There may also be the assumption that people are capable of being intrinsically motivated by reason, so that if we can make a rational case for the ways of life we value, then others (or at least some others; well, maybe just other philosophers) can thereby be motivated to share those ways of life, and that we would be rationally justified in so persuading them.

If the theory I have been sketching is correct, then none of these claims is sound. The connection between positive value and any other content of experience or focus of motivation is contingent. We have nothing stronger on which to take a stand except the current contingencies of our own psychology. And those can change.

Such changes may double the vulnerability of what we care about. There is the vulnerability expressed by Yeats: "Man is in love and loves what vanishes, What more is there to say?"[9] Unfortunately, there is more to say, specifically, though much less poetically, "Man is in love, and he may cease to love what he now loves, and thus what he now loves may vanish."

Let me illustrate with something I care about—other forms of life and wilderness areas. It is certainly possible to have a positive affective response to these primarily as a result of seeing them in the context of, let us say, Darwinian theory. Many have shared Darwin's sense that "there is grandeur in this view of life. . . ."[10] Nevertheless, I suspect such responses would not be very strong in the absence of positive affect gained from direct experiences of wild creatures and wild places. And there is the real vulnerability—as fewer and fewer urbanized people have any opportunity for such experiences, the fate of wild things may become a matter of indifference. The probabilities are running that way. Indeed, as a theoretical possibility, I could change in that way, though that now seems unimaginable.

I can imagine a very urbanized future. In such a future, there may be swarms of humans, and many of them may have lives filled with positive affect, though none of that affect would be associated with anything wild. Perhaps a post-Darwinian sensibility can come to see this change as just one more shift in the contingencies of life (once there were dinosaurs and their ways of life; now there are some wilderness lovers; later there will be lovers of the purely urban) and view this possibility with the same positive affect of mild amusement and detachment.

Were there but world enough and time, this is a stance I could take. If it were merely a matter of adding to the variety of lives that individuals find satisfactory, each in his or her own way, I would have no quarrel. I do not deplore the urban sensibility of a Samuel Johnson ("When a man is tired of London, he is tired of life; for there is in London *all* that life can afford"[11]). But there is not world enough; expansion of urban life is at the expense of wild areas, and expansion of the urban sensibility can only accelerate that process.

We are in the area of concern with the impact of lives on other lives, and that again raises ethical issues I am bracketing for now. If we concentrate on what makes a life a good life for the creature whose life it is, we are left with something of a double vision. In one sense, all good lives are the same—all are lives with instances of positive affect. Such affect is the only intrinsic good. This good is relative only in the sense that the instances of it can only exist in the experiences of individuals. But my positive affect and yours and that of a sloth are good in exactly the same way.

On the other hand, most instances of positive affect are caused by specific kinds of experiences with their own distinctive nonaffective contents that become the focus of ongoing motivation. In this sense, there are many different kinds of good life, and what is good for one individual may not be good for another.

Finally, we may on occasion reflect on—have an image of—these many different kinds of lives, and only some of those images will, for any given individual, produce positive affect that will lead him or her to pronounce *that* a good life in the sense that he or she would be motivated to lead such a life.

Only some lives could be a good life for me as I am now constituted. When I sum up a life as a possible answer to the question, How should I lead my life?, I am standing, and must be standing, on my own affective responses. This does not give an answer to the question, How should we human beings lead our lives?, and thus may not seem a very strong place to stand, but what my theory tells me is that it is the best we have, and it is at least as strong as where anyone else is standing. We must, perforce, lead our lives under the form of contingency.

6

REASONS, NORMS, COGNITION, AND AFFECT

In the previous chapter, I developed the implications of RET's theory of intrinsic value for an answer to the question, What constitutes a good life for the creature whose life it is? RET's answer is that the overall intrinsic value of a life is a summation of positive hedonic tone (suitably balanced against a summation of negative hedonic tone). Hedonic tone, positive or negative, is only contingently connected with any other contents of experience; thus, while the causal sources of intrinsic value may vary enormously among individuals, the actual value-constituting property (hedonic tone) is the same across this variety of lives, and in this sense all good lives are the same.

For many, however, the question, What is the good life? is the supremely ethical question, and it is often rephrased as, How ought I to lead my life?—thus making it a normative issue. Such standard associations are bound to generate resistance to my claim that intrinsic value (positive or negative) is not as such normative.

In addition to these associations with the ethical, there are equally strong associations between the concept of intrinsic value and sundry concepts of the reasonable, the rational, and above all with the notion and practice of giving reasons for our actions. Surely, one might insist, to say that something is intrinsically good is to give a reason, perhaps even the ultimate reason, for pursuing or promoting or defending that something. And the giving of reasons is, again, a normative activity.

141

INTRINSIC VALUE AND REASONS

Let me start the debate with the following challenge: If RET's theory of value has no direct implications for how we should lead our lives, then why would any such so-called value matter?

A good beginning is to note that there is a kind of "mattering" that has to do with intrinsic qualities of experience. It is implausible to assume that all mattering has to do with desire, pursuit, choice, and the future. Surely all that kind of mattering must at some time come to fruition in the quality of what we have now, and sometimes such intrinsically good experiences are a pure gift, to be accepted as such. So of course intrinsically positive hedonic tone matters, just because it is good.

Conceptions of value tend to be influenced by conflicting conceptions of the role of value. The primary role of intrinsic value, I claim, is to bring good into the lives of creatures. This is not a role that value plays as any sort of agent, nor is it a role that was assigned to value, or planned, or intended. It just happened, as one of the sheer gifts of nature. (Any gratitude for this gift would require, not only a questionable personification, but also an overlooking of the fact that nature has also provided us with much intrinsic disvalue.) This role of value is certainly historically prior to and independent of any role as an intersubjective standard, or as a social norm, or as a resolver of disputes.

Let us next consider a more strenuous, action-oriented kind of mattering. I have defended an empirically constrained theory that claims that Reward Events (instances of positive hedonic tone) play a major causal role in determining what we are motivated to do, and that they are the only events that are (in creatures that are Reward Event Systems) intrinsically (positively) motivating (motivating in their own right). So they matter that way, too.

Of course, the causal role of intrinsic value can lead to choices or preferences that may not be very intelligible or rational in terms of the (varying) normative standards often associated with those terms. As I argued earlier, intrinsic value does not as such tell us what we ought to do or what we have reason to do.

There might be some exceptions to this claim if we had a thoroughly naturalized conception of reasons for action that aimed to show how reasons actually cause actions, thus making the role of reasons an empirical question. The most purely cognitive model would claim that reasons are beliefs and that—at least sometimes—a belief as such can directly cause action. (More plausibly, a reason would be a well-grounded belief—a belief generated by methods or mechanisms that are reliably truth-producing.) This model would make us rational beings in the purest sense of the term. I have argued that the psychological and neuropsychological evidence suggests that this model is mistaken, that belief as such does not cause action. Furthermore, even if there should be such cases, if value is constituted by noncognitive affect, then these would be cases in which value played no causal role.

A more usual model sees reasons for action as combinations of beliefs and desires. This model makes reasons for action cognitive in that extended sense that applies to any psychological state with intentional content. I have argued that a belief-desire model is seriously incomplete and that an adequate psychological model needs to take account of the key causal role of affect, which has no intentional content and is thus strictly noncognitive. In RET, affect in itself—not a thought of or belief about affect—plays this causal role.

Might we then develop an extended model of reasons for action that includes an appropriate combination of belief, desire, and affect? Such an extension of the term 'reason' would be seriously misleading. The term has strong cognitive associations; if it were used to cover a complex that included not only desires but also a key noncognitive component, then it would continue to perpetuate a view of ourselves as highly rational beings, when in fact the actual empirical model undermines that view in anything like its traditional sense.

If one has a thoroughly naturalized, causal conception of reasons for actions, it then becomes a complex empirical question as to which instances of intrinsic value (if any) generate or help to constitute such reasons and for which creatures.

Reasons naturalized in a purely causal way would not, as such, carry normative implications. But the concept of reasons has always tended to suggest a combination of both causes of and rationalizations for actions. Since Freud, a rationalization need not be seen as strongly normative, but at a minimum it has implied that we can (or can seem to) make sense of the action in a way that enables us to see the agent as a rational being. And there always hovers in the background, both in commonsense and, especially, in many philosophical theories, the implicit norm that we should above all aim to be rational.

Such normative implications have at best an uneasy fit with any causal conception of reasons. Perhaps the closest fit would be in the territory of means-ends rationality. Surely a core sense of practical reason would involve using effective means in pursuit of one's ends. Indeed, unless a creature operated that way on the whole (whether by conscious deliberation or not), it would be a poor candidate for continued survival.

This concession, which should be made by any naturalist, does not introduce full-blown normative prudence, which has to do with maximizing advantage over the course of an entire life. As we have seen, even a philosopher who develops an ethical theory on the basis of "rational decision theory" can claim that we have a reason to be prudent with respect to our future advantage only if we now have a preference for our future advantage (Gauthier 1986). Once reasons become normative, they become highly contested. If this is true even concerning means-end rationality—or what is often called strategic rationality—in which ends are simply taken as a given, how much more it is likely to be the case when the concept of reasons is extended to ends themselves.

Such an extension is made by the claim that if something has intrinsic value, then it must be a reason for acting. This has an understandable and almost intuitive plausibility. If something is intrinsically good—good in its own right—then surely this is an excellent (the most excellent) reason for making it an end. And surely we ought to pursue the good and shun the bad. And yet . . .

If the intrinsic good identified by a theorist as that which we ought to pursue is some ideal that even the theorist does not suppose is actually pursued in all cases, and thus in many cases may not be the cause of action, then the normative conception of reason will dominate over the causal, leaving the problems of how such reasons can become causes and whether their doing so is consistent with a naturalistic theory of the causes of action.

Even if there is a plausible naturalization of reasons or norms as real properties operating causally in human life, these are likely to be complex, social, relational properties. And if—as I have argued—intrinsic value is an intrinsic property, then it cannot be constituted by such relational properties.

It has perhaps been assumed that only if we tie value to reasons (and thereby to rationality) can we put it on a sound common basis not subject to the vagaries of feeling and sentiment. But conceptions of reasons, particularly when related to ends, are subject to all the pressures of competing ideologies, in ways that may distort our understanding of intrinsic value.

The point can be illustrated by considering the contemporary debate among theorists of value as to whether intrinsic value is "agent neutral" or "agent relative."[1] I believe this debate has been structured by the assumption that if value is agent neutral, then it must follow that value is thereby a reason for any agent to act and may even, in the absence of contrary reasons, oblige any agent to act, whereas if value is agent-relative, it only provides a reason for that particular agent to act.

Suppose a creature is experiencing intense pain. If we say that the experience is painful for that creature, and thus bad for that creature, this can be interpreted in two different ways. According to any theory, such as RET, that makes intrinsic value an intrinsic property, the creature's pain is bad (*simpliciter*), and that it is bad is an objective truth—true for all. Thus, in saying that the pain is bad for the creature, we are simply locating[2] the pain and the intrinsic badness. By contrast, a relational-property theory of intrinsic value might say that the badness of the pain is constituted by the aversive reaction of the creature to the pain, and if (which is a possibility) no other creature has any such aversive reaction to that instance of pain, then the pain is only bad for that creature, in the stronger sense that relativizes value to particular individuals. For those not experiencing the pain, the only truth to be acknowledged is not that the creature experiencing the pain is undergoing a bad experience (full stop), but that the creature is undergoing an experience that is bad for it.

Now, suppose that one assumes that it is a conceptual truth that intrinsic value (disvalue) provides a reason for acting, which in the absence of countervailing reasons might even be a conclusive reason. Suppose also that one sees moral judgments as providing at least a species of reasons for action, and that one may even hope to show that they can provide conclusive reasons; in other words, one makes rationality (or having reasons) the central normative term in one's ethical theory.

If one accepted all of these suppositions, then one would believe that if one acknowledges that the pain of a creature is bad in a fully nonrelative sense, one must thereby acknowledge that not only does the creature have a reason to do something about its pain, but *so does any other agent*. Indeed, given additional conditions (absence of countervailing reasons and so on) one might even be obligated to do something about that creature's pain, whether one was in any way responsible for its being in pain, or had violated its rights, or the like.

Many ethical theorists might find these conclusions congenial, but many others would not. Thus, the former might believe they must defend an agent-neutral view of intrinsic value, while the latter would be equally convinced that intrinsic value had better be agent-relative or the floodgates will open and we will drown in obligations.

We can, I believe, gain a far more honest and open-minded view of where there are actual instances of intrinsic value, in both human and nonhuman lives, if we sever the presumed conceptual connections between intrinsic value and reasons or norms.

In addition, if we tie value to reasons, and if we wish to make the case that at least sometimes value/reasons play a real, causal motivational role in our lives, these assumptions are likely to bias our causal picture toward the cognitive, whether narrowly or broadly conceived. And that bias, as I have argued, may well lead us to miss key causal aspects of our psychology.

In sum, there are a number of good theoretical reasons for saying that intrinsic value—the intrinsically good—is not normative. In addition to such reasons of theory, I also have argued that any relational-property theory of value mischaracterizes the one natural property that is intrinsically good in its own right.

REASONS AND ETHICS

Even if we do not tie intrinsic value conceptually to reasons or norms, surely the good must be relevant to norms, particularly to norms of ethics or morality. The fact that we can, causally, produce either intrinsic value or intrinsic disvalue in other lives cannot be morally irrelevant.

The point is sound, but does not take us very far. There are strongly defended theories that would insist that there is only a small range of the good and the bad, out of all its actual instances, that is relevant to what an individual agent ought to do or has a moral obligation to be concerned with. If, the argument goes, we had to monitor and adjust our actions in terms of their full long-term potential for producing or preventing the good or bad, that would be exhausting if not impossible and would leave us no room to lead our individual lives.[3]

To generalize, it is a long-standing and much-contested issue in ethics as to how intrinsic good and bad matter to ethics, particularly how the good and the bad in the lives of others should matter to an agent. What is the pain of the stranger to me? This debate really presupposes that there is good and bad. It does not clarify the issues to try to settle the debate by a prior structuring of one's theory of intrinsic value, making it either agent-neutral or agent-relative.

Where the debate has often focused is on the nature of reasons. A causal orientation will tend to tie the having of a reason to actual motivation; this is often labeled an "internalist" theory of reasons. If we are to be seriously causal, however, we should be open to different possibilities concerning what causes us to do the things we do. Tying a causal picture to reasons may bias theories toward cognitive causes. If, for example, an adequate account of motivation has to bring in psychological mechanisms such as sympathy, and if these mechanisms essentially involve noncognitive aspects of our psychology, then focusing on reasons may rule out a priori what is really occurring. If, instead, the concept of reasons is extended to cover all causal aspects, a misleading refusal to acknowledge the role of the noncognitive could result.

A normative conception of reasons that does not tie reasons conceptually to motivation (an "externalist" theory) would avoid these problems, but the normative dimension of reasons, as a conceptual tool in ethical theory, has its own difficulties. Perhaps the best way to spell out these difficulties, and to focus my own objections to the use of 'rational' or 'reasons' as a central term in ethical theory, is to examine in detail the theories of Gibbard and Brandt.

Gibbard's (1990) "norm-expressivistic analysis" of rationality and his theory of "normative judgment" exploit "devices pioneered by such ethical noncognitivists as A. J. Ayer, Charles Stevenson, and R. M. Hare" (vii). Gibbard's aim is to "naturalize" norms and to fit the "giving of reasons" and the "accepting of norms" into a fully naturalized psychology. I have a great deal of sympathy with these aims, but I think Gibbard's terminological choices are misleading.

The key to our differences may lie in the fact that Gibbard sees as central to his project capturing "what the term 'rational' means" (vii). By contrast, I have certain skeptical suspicions that what people mean by "rational" or "giving reasons" may be seriously misleading as to the actual psychology of those practices. Gibbard and I are both interested in what is really going on psychologically, but there may be (depending on what is going on) good reasons for not labeling such activities the "giving of reasons" or calling the outcomes endorsed by such activities the "rational thing to do or to feel."

"To think something rational," Gibbard says, "is to accept norms that permit it," and a norm is "a possible rule or prescription, expressible by an imperative" (46). In the spirit of traditional noncognitive analyses, Gibbard then goes on to emphasize that his analysis is "a hypothesis about what it is to *think* or *believe* something rational, to *regard* it as rational, to *consider* it rational" (46). The implication is clear that "if we want to decide what really *is* rational, we shall have to settle what norms to accept ourselves—for that is what it is to form an opinion as to the rationality of something" (47). In applying this framework of analysis to ethics, Gibbard goes on to introduce a key role for moral emotions, saying that "moral norms in particular are norms for the rationality of guilt and resentment" (47).[4]

To naturalize his conception of rationality, Gibbard must naturalize what it is to accept a norm and place acceptance within a wider biological perspective. (This insistence on placing us in an evolutionary perspective is one of the strengths of his theory.)

> If there is such a thing as governance by norms, there must be psychic mechanisms that accomplish it, and we can ask about their biological function. That function, I want to suggest, is to *coordinate*. Accepting a norm and being in its grip manifest two different systems of coordination. Of these, the capacity to accept norms is peculiarly human and depends on language. (61)

From this wider biological perspective, Gibbard is willing to say that in a "limited sense" not only do we have norms but so do "various beasts" (70). His claim is grounded in the plausible assumption that we have evolved a capacity to "accept norms" and should thus expect to find limited analogues in other creatures. Thus, he says that some other creatures also *internalize* norms, and he explicates internalization as follows:

By the norm itself, I suggest, we should mean a prescription or imperative that gives the rule a sophisticated observer could formulate. The imperative is a formulation of a pattern which, in effect, controls the organism's behavior. (70)

[W]here norm N prescribes a certain behavioral pattern B, an organism *internalizes* N if and only if it has a motivational tendency, of the kind I have picked out, to act on pattern B. . . . examples are united by purposes of coordination. Tendencies to act on the pattern (or propensities to acquire those tendencies when growing up exposed to the pattern) constitute biological adaptations for coordination. (71)

We are thus led to see norms as coordination devices that have evolved in social creatures; this is a very plausible initial naturalization of norms.

What, then, according to Gibbard, is distinctive about the human case? How does the acceptance of norms differ from or go beyond the mere internalization of norms? The key is the use of language to rehearse and to coordinate our avowals and actions; the mechanisms involve mutual influence and a responsiveness to demands for consistency. Thus, the state of accepting a norm "is identified by its place in a syndrome produced by the language-infused system of coordination peculiar to human beings" (75). More precisely, accepting a norm is *"whatever psychic state* [my emphasis], if any, gives rise to the syndrome . . ." (75).

Gibbard is describing what are unquestionably common human practices. He has offered a biological naturalization of these practices, and he also admits that in the individual case such practices must work through "whatever psychic state" is playing this causal role.

Why, then, tie these practices to the concepts of rationality and the giving of reasons? It is not just because that is what humans have, on the whole, called such practices, though that is part of Gibbard's case. His theoretical case rests on several claims. There is his claim that the practices involve demands for consistency and that we are responsive to such demands. And consistency (presumably logical consistency) is indeed a component of rationality in a full-blown cognitive sense.

Gibbard also makes the following claim, which alludes to a wider range of psychological mechanisms:

[T]he psychic states and processes I have depicted—the acceptance of norms, and normative control of action and emotion—do not fit neatly into the traditional psychologists' categories of cognition, affect, and conation.

> The capacities involved, though, do fit a traditional conception of the faculty of reason. They involve the use of language, demands for consistency, and a limited governance of action and emotion. This last, indeed, may be what psychologists sometimes call "rational control." (80)

This case is plausible, and I must deal with it piece by piece. First, consistency certainly is a cognitive virtue—a virtue of rationality. Perhaps a theory of what goes on in our recognition of logical consistency (or, for that matter, the truths of logic and mathematics) might call that in question, but I have no wish to contest it. I would only note that we probably do not have a fully adequate psychological theory of that process, and thus that this domain of the normative is by no means fully naturalized.

Ethical norms, however—despite Kant's notorious attempt to prove otherwise—involve far more than *formal* consistency. Consistency is just one minimal constraint on the process of normative discussion.

What else, then, is going on in such discussion? Granted, it is what we call giving reasons, but Gibbard himself says that the actual psychological processes do not fit neatly into traditional psychological categories of cognition, affect, and conation. It is not that Gibbard is offering an alternative psychological theory that would challenge those traditional categories. Rather, the point seems to be that this complex process of persuasion and governance engages all of these aspects of our psychology and in that sense is not a purely cognitive process. The mere giving of evidence and establishing the empirical facts of a case is not, one presumes, sufficient.

The process does involve the use of language, but as noncognitivists such as Stevenson have emphasized, many uses of language do not appeal solely to our rationality, but also to emotion and affect. We can call the latter modes of influence giving reasons, but if they are primarily noncognitive processes, this characterization seems misleading.

There is also, Gibbard says, the "governance of action and emotion"; this is the territory of actual causal control of motivation and action. Calling this control "rational control" strongly suggests that this control relies on our cognitive capacities. Gibbard does say that we are "responsive" to demands for consistency, but even here we are not sure exactly how this works. Does a recognition of inconsistency alone cause us to change our beliefs? Or does the influence of cognitive dissonance, a topic much discussed by psychologists, perhaps require affective associations?

Once we go beyond the influence of formal consistency (or inconsistency), is it enough for Gibbard, in his discussion of the key process of accepting a norm, to handwave toward "whatever psychic state" gives rise to this syndrome of avowal and governance? If, as I have been arguing, no cognitive content as such can motivate, but only content contingently associated with noncognitive affect, then is it not misleading to call this process the giving of reasons? This labeling may not only mislead us as to what is really occurring, but also perpetuate an ideology of humans as rational beings.

Gibbard's own naturalization project is grounded biologically and makes empirical appeal to careful sociological descriptions of the processes of normative deliberation. What I am suggesting is that we also need a psychological theory of what is occurring, and that this theory should control the terms we use to describe the processes.[5]

In this respect, my theory is methodologically closer to that of Brandt. Brandt (1979) criticizes any appeal to "linguistic intuitions," and proposes instead a "reforming definition" of the term 'rational.' Brandt makes this reformed concept of the rational the central term in his theory, and then uses it to define the good and the right. One of the key things "we *want to know*, for purposes of decision making," says Brandt, "is how far actions, desires, and moral systems can be criticized by appeal to facts and observations. . . . With this question in mind, I shall pre-empt the term 'rational' to refer to actions, desires, or moral systems which survive maximal criticism and correction by facts and logic" (10).

This move is a step in the right direction. Brandt would not include any causal influence of noncognitive affect in that which constitutes the rationality of desire or action or in that which constitutes reasons for action. Rationality is restricted to the territory of the cognitive.

Within this territory, Brandt also makes an important distinction:

> [A person's action is] rational to a first approximation, if and only if it is what he would have done if all the mechanisms determining action except for his desires and aversions (which are taken as they are)—that is, the *cognitive inputs* influencing decisions/action—had been optimal as far as possible. . . . if and only if every item of *relevant available* information is present to awareness, vividly, at the focus of attention, or with an equal share of attention. (11)

This position is familiar. The only way, according to Hume, that we can sensibly speak of an action being rational or irrational is if the beliefs contributing causally to the action are rational. Any desire, particularly any ultimate desire (desire for an ultimate end), cannot as such be either rational or irrational. More precisely, Hume (1978) puts it this way:

> [I]t is only in two senses that any affection can be called unreasonable. First, when a passion such as hope or fear, grief or joy, despair or security, is founded on the supposition of the existence of objects which really do not exist. Secondly, when in exerting any passion in action, we choose means insufficient for the designed end, and deceive ourselves in our judgment of causes and effects. When a passion is neither founded on false suppositions, nor chooses means insufficient for the end, the understanding can neither justify nor condemn it. (416)

I find Hume's claim sound, at least in the sense that restricting rationality, in any primary sense, to the territory of belief is probably the least misleading way to use this very cognitive term. One can then extend the term to action and passion in the way indicated. For many, however, restricting the term 'rational' in this way has not seemed adequate for capturing our practices of criticism or our ordinary ways of describing those practices; nor does it allow for rational criticism of ultimate ends.

Brandt does extend the term 'rational' to desires and aversions. A desire or aversion is rational "if and only if it is what it would have been had the person undergone *cognitive psychotherapy*" (11). This cognitive psychotherapy is Brandt's well-known conception of a "process of confronting desires with relevant information, by repeatedly representing it, in an ideally vivid way, and at an appropriate time" (113).

While Brandt's conception of cognitive psychotherapy involves a causal sense of relevance, it is important to note that it is not the sort of extended sense used by noncognitivists such as Stevenson, who would count as relevant any belief that causally affects desire or action, whether that effect is through emotive overtones, affective associations, or what have you. Brandt characterizes 'relevant' as follows:

> We need to restrict further the kind of information that qualifies as 'relevant,' in order to guarantee that the effectiveness of the information *is a function of its content* [my emphasis]. If every time I thought of having a martini, I made myself go through the multiplication tables for five minutes, the valence of a martini might well decline. But obviously the desire for a martini is not misdirected simply if it fails to survive

confrontation with the multiplication table in this way. Any desire would be discouraged by this procedure. We want to say that a thought is functioning properly in the criticism of desires only if its effect is not one its occurrence would have on any desire, and only if its effect is a function of its content. It must be a thought in some fairly restricted way about the thing desired; for instance, a thought about the expectable effects of the thing, or about the kind of thing it is, or about how well one would like it if it happened, and so on. (112)

Several comments are in order. First, the notion of a belief causing something by virtue of its content is at the center of much contemporary debate in the cognitive sciences: Can we naturalize semantic causation? This is an issue even with respect to evidential relevance, or to how one belief influences other beliefs. From this perspective, Brandt's concern with semantic causation of desires may not seem a departure from semantic causation of beliefs; it is not to be dismissed as a switch from logical relations to causal relations. If semantic causation is common to both change of belief and change of desire, this can be the basis of an argument for the extension of the term 'rational' to desires that have undergone this process of semantic causation; perhaps how we rationally make up our minds about a belief is not that different from how we rationally make up our minds about desire and action.

A closer look, however, may raise some questions. Some of the "content" that Brandt mentions is about the "expectable effects" of a thing. The rationality of one's beliefs about expectable effects can be seen as a part of our overall rationality with respect to cause and effect. But belief that thing A will have effect B, no matter how rational that belief, may make no difference at all to desire or action unless we care about B (a point Gauthier made in his discussion of prudence). So the real focus is ultimately on thoughts about "the kind of thing it is," or "how well one would like it if it happened."

We can now deal with a key empirical issue. "The claim," says Brandt, "is that relevant available information, if confronted on repeated occasions, affects our desires" (112). This effect is to be caused by content. Furthermore, reflecting on content is to be *"value-free reflection"* (113); the reflection's being value-free is essential for Brandt's naturalization project. In brief, the characterization of the possible object of desire should be a just-the-facts characterization available to any disinterested observer.

But can such neutral content, in itself, cause desire or a change in desire? Consider first the content focused on "the kind of thing it is." What I have been arguing is that any such content does not in itself motivate; only when intrinsically neutral content is contingently associated with affect (which is intrinsically motivating) does it become the object (or as I have called it, the focus) of motivation.

I have even suggested that associations of affect are required if the thought of such affect (of pleasure or enjoyment), which is what Brandt has in mind in speaking of "how well one would like it if it happened," is to be motivating. Belief that one will experience pleasure (or pain) may not be able, as such, to motivate; even these thoughts or beliefs may have to be associated with present actual affect (which is not itself a thought or belief) in order to motivate or to have any impact on desire and action. (I should remind the reader that Brandt does not agree with my characterization of pleasure; for him, pleasure is defined in motivational terms.)

These are empirical claims, and thus my disagreements with Brandt (unlike my disagreements with Gibbard) are primarily empirical. If, as Brandt seems to claim, semantic content as such, as embodied in beliefs, can directly cause changes in desire and thus in actions, then this causation is indeed cognitive, and if these beliefs are themselves rational—if, in Brandt's terms, these cognitive inputs have been formed on the basis of all relevant available information—then this would plausibly count as acting for reasons or as constituting an instance of rational action.

But is Brandt's model a plausible causal model, and is it what Brandt himself believes? In correspondence with Brandt, I have been led to believe that he would not accept the possibility of causation by belief alone (of the sort, for example, defended by Nagel 1970, 1986). And yet Brandt does cite, as supporting evidence for his view, the apparent successes of certain forms of therapy in altering desires (e.g., for alcohol) by encouraging thoughts *of* aversive reactions (Brandt 1979, 1992). "Rehearsal of the unpleasant effects of some state of affairs can," Brandt says, "reduce the desire for it" (1992, 19). His fuller characterization of this process is instructive:

> So, if one is an alcoholic, and wants to get rid of the desire, one thing to do is dwell on the bad consequences at times when one is tempted to drink, and get the benefit of the association. Failure to do this is a kind of *cognitive* [my emphasis] mistake, failure to represent the facts. (19)

Brandt does emphasize that such representation of the facts must be "vivid" to be causally effective, but such vividness cannot be more than having the relevant facts clearly in focus now, if the causation is to be due to the content. What cannot be going on—and what I suspect is going on—is that the contents are contingently associated with affect, and it is the latter that is the key to making those contents causally effective.

In summary, I would say that if Brandt is empirically correct, then his suggested reforming definition of 'rational' is plausible and would not be causally misleading. But if my theory of motivation is on the whole correct, and if in particular there is no causation of motivation or desire by the semantic content of belief as such, then Brandt's reforming definition should be rejected, since it would give the wrong answer to Brandt's own question as to "how far actions, desires, and moral systems can be criticized [that is, effectively changed] by appeal to facts and observations [as such]" (1979, 10), particularly when that question focuses on ultimate desires for those ends we want for their own sake.[6]

Finally, I would suggest that debates over how to define 'rational' are not just philosophers' terminological disputes. Much more is at stake. We are all concerned with how or whether people come to accept norms, as well as with which norms they accept. This concern looms particularly large in a consideration of how young people are brought into a moral community—how they come to accept its norms. If we have the wrong psychological theory about what must occur, we will be ineffective and will not understand when the process fails to work.

For example, what kind of affective bonding (if any) must be in place between an adult norm-giver and a young potential acceptor of those norms? May it make a great difference which experiences and activities at an early age become associated with positive affect or negative affect? Is instruction (in a more strictly cognitive sense) enough?

The naturalistic spirit of Brandt and Gibbard is most congenial to me. I have been arguing that we do need to go a layer down in our neuropsychology, and that the motivational theory that emerges at that level may either modify or at least put in a different perspective their higher-level generalizations about how we humans work and carry on our practices. My own conclusions are probably more radical and skeptical than are theirs. Our differences may be due primarily to differences about empirical issues, though that remains to be seen. It is a further project to apply RET to an ethics for contingent creatures.

RET defends a solid realism about intrinsic value; there are real natural properties (positive and negative hedonic tone) that *are* good or bad. This is a true description of these qualities of experience, but it is not a normative truth. Whether there are normative truths or ethical truths is, I suspect, more questionable.

I can make the following brief suggestion in reply to my own acknowledgment that in some sense intrinsic value must be relevant to norms and particularly to ethical norms. If (as I have argued is the case for Reward Events) there are events that are both intrinsically good and intrinsically motivating, then on almost any plausible ethical view these events are bound to play a role, and in that sense they are bound to be relevant. On the other hand, it would not follow that the relevance is any sort of logical relevance grounded in cognitive content. According to RET, such cognitive grounding of relevance is unlikely to be the case. Thus, in the spirit of my criticism of the use of the term 'rational' in ethical theory, it may turn out that in ethics we should not speak of relevance but of causal roles, as we track the many ways in which positive (and negative) affect appear in individual lives.

For many, replacing "relevance" with "causal roles" may seem to eliminate the genuinely normative. It may, however, be the only way we can naturalize the normative and fit it into an overall view of ourselves as natural, contingent creatures.

THE NATURALISTIC FALLACY REVISITED

It will no doubt have been noted that throughout my discussions I have used the terms 'positive affect,' 'positive hedonic tone,' 'pleasure,' and 'positive value' or 'good' as equivalent descriptions for certain intrinsic qualities of experience. The presumed equivalence of the first three terms depends on a regimenting of the term 'affect' (which is often used in the psychological literature to cover a wider range of phenomena, such as emotions) and on the success of the arguments for my intrinsic-quality characterization of pleasure.

The last two terms—'positive value' and 'goodness' (to use the noun form)—are likely to raise distinct alarm signals. In using, for example, 'pleasure' and 'intrinsic value' or 'goodness' in this equivalent way, am I not guilty of committing the naturalistic fallacy?

The term 'naturalistic fallacy' has its own history and by now has been used to refer not only to the original charge formulated by Moore (1903) but to a range of issues from the presumed gap between "is" and "ought" to the possibility of realism in ethics. I will make no attempt to deal with all these issues, nor with the extensive literature they have generated. I will instead focus on those interpretations of the fallacy that are either relevant to my project or are (perhaps mistakenly) assumed to be relevant.

The initial point to be made is that I have been developing a theory of *nonmoral* value. I have argued that the intrinsic value that is an intrinsic quality of experience is not normative; it carries no obvious implications for what we ought to do. The goodness of the experience does not involve some odd quality of "to-be-pursuedness"; if the motivational theory of RET is correct, it does involve "is-pursuedness," but this is due to contingent causal connections. I am not, therefore, making any claim about how one can go from assertions about the goodness of experience to assertions about what we ought to do. I offer no theory of ethics. If there is a gap between is and ought, I make no claim to have bridged it.

I have claimed that insofar as an experience is pleasant, it is thereby good—the quality of pleasure is the intrinsic positive value. And since pleasure is a natural property, so is this nonmoral value—this goodness. These are precisely the kinds of claims that were Moore's target.

It has long been recognized (see Frankena 1939) that Moore's arguments do not identify any formal logical fallacy. Those who commit the naturalistic fallacy have either (Moore's view) mistaken a natural property (pleasure) for a distinct nonnatural property (goodness) or have confused a descriptive use of language ("This is pleasant") with an evaluative use ("This is good"). Many contemporary ethical realists would reject any claim that this dichotomy exhausts the possibilities, but since their realisms are usually naturalistic, they would also reject any claim that a theory that interprets value properties (being nonmorally good) and ethical properties (being morally good, being right, and so on) as being real natural properties must thereby commit some fallacy.

Have I made a mistake about properties or about language? RET claims that we can identify in experience a distinct intrinsic quality of positive hedonic tone (pleasure) and that referring to this quality (as in describing an experience as pleasant) gives a correct description of the experience. Describing the experience as positive is part of this correct description, and in this context, that is equivalent to describing it as good. The point may be more obvious in the parallel cases of negative qualities. Consider an experience (as in severe depression) of pure awfulness—of extremely negative hedonic tone. Consider this series of descriptions: It's awful; It's terrible; It's really bad. Have we, in this series, jumped some gap from the descriptive to the evaluative, much less from "is" to "ought"? On the contrary, if you describe an experience as one of extreme pain or suffering, you thereby describe it as bad. And if you describe an experience as pleasant or euphoric, you thereby describe it as good. These are correct descriptions of experiences, and the qualities ascribed to the experiences are thoroughly natural.

I do not claim that these uses of the terms 'good' and 'bad' are their only uses; many uses may carry ethical or normative implications, and ordinary language does not make clean distinctions among uses. I do claim that in this fundamental descriptive use, the terms identify intrinsic qualities of experience. These qualities (and, I believe, only these qualities) make experiences intrinsically good or bad.

The disagreement remains as to whether the properties of pleasure or of pain are intrinsic qualities or relational properties, and thus as to whether the pleasantness or goodness of an experience—or the awfulness or badness—are intrinsic qualities or are, instead, relational properties such as reactions *to* the experiences. These are quarrels within naturalism; none of these theories commits any naturalistic fallacy, though many of the theories have not been extended to an explicit theory of value.

Given the wide range of interpretations of the so-called naturalistic fallacy, I do not suppose that this brief reply can satisfy all critics. I can only reassert my fundamental claim that many experiences really are intrinsically pleasant or painful, that is, intrinsically positive or negative, that is, intrinsically good or bad.

7

HEDONISM, IDEOLOGY, AND TEMPERAMENT

There are both cultural and theoretical reasons why this is a difficult time to defend hedonism. It is a theory that allows intrinsic value to run with some fairly disreputable company, and when the value is claimed to be an intrinsic, noncognitive quality of conscious experience, this position goes against the grain of much contemporary philosophy of mind and cognitive science, with their emphases on informational states or states with intentional content. There is also a preference, among many philosophers and psychologists, for treating mental states in terms of their relational properties, whether this is seen as a commitment to functionalism, or operational definitions, or externalism, or a kind of internal connectionism. Qualia (phenomenal qualities) of any kind have always been a nuisance. Finally, there is the lingering suspicion that confining the intrinsically good to pleasure trivializes intrinsic value. The intrinsically good should somehow be a deep fact, at least about us, if not about the universe.

I have at least indirectly spoken to these concerns at various points throughout this book, but these are powerful currents in the contemporary scene, and a more direct reply will at least place my theory in a wider context, if not satisfy all critics.

The Essential Innocence of Pleasure

Reward Events can be triggered directly in the brain by electrical stimulation; this fact can arouse Orwellian qualms, particularly in philosophers, and has generated those Experience Machine fantasies that have been deployed as counterintuitions against any theory that confines intrinsic value to internal qualities of experience. But Reward Events can also be triggered directly by drugs, such as cocaine; furthermore, this triggering is, according to RET, a direct triggering of intrinsic value. This claim could raise qualms across the social spectrum. Surely, the thought may go, the great social problem of our times is the search for immediate pleasure. What is destroying lives is the inability to postpone gratification. (It is left a bit vague as to whether the needed ability is to postpone gratification *forever.*) And could anything in those experiences (fill in here a vivid picture of an inner-city crack house) be intrinsically good, much less the only intrinsic good?

A good bit of the concern so expressed is of course generated by the impact of the drug user on other lives. This is a genuine concern and would no doubt loom large in any moral assessment of particular methods for generating Reward Events. Those methods, in addition to generating intrinsic value, may well play a causal role in generating much intrinsic disvalue. In addition—depending on one's moral theory—they might be condemned in other moral terms, such as the violation of rights. (A corollary of my view that intrinsic value is not normative is that hedonism does not entail some form of utilitarianism.)

In addition, there is a well-founded concern that getting caught up in drug addiction can wreck the drug user's own life. This method of generating Reward Events can also generate a great deal of intrinsic disvalue for the user.

But why should these complex causal and social facts call in question the intrinsic value of the pleasure generated by such means? It has long been recognized that activities may have multiple effects, some good and some bad. Why should it be any different in these cases? Why can we not accept the tolerant and clear-headed perspective of David Hume, who wrote, "If the unlimited use of strong liquors, for instance, no more impaired health or the faculties of mind and body than the use of air or water, it would not be a whit more vicious or blameable."[1] Condemning the pleasure generated by drug use is surely unwarranted guilt by association. Even with respect to the drug-user's whole life, particularly those cases held up as cautionary examples, is it really an honest portrayal or diagnosis to say that the trouble with these lives is that they have contained too much pleasure?

The intrinsically good, as the intrinsic natural property of positive hedonic tone, has only contingent associations (causal or otherwise) with any other natural properties, and this contingency of association of course allows it to be present in all sorts of company, reputable and otherwise. These possibilities in no way alter its intrinsic goodness; pleasure is not a moral agent that can be blamed for the company it keeps. Here we may be influenced by an ideology of value, at least as old as Plato, that has seen The Good as somehow our guide to life, which can authoritatively tell us what to do. This seductive personification should be resisted.

There may also be other influences at work, beyond a concern not to be seen endorsing anything connected with drugs. There are cultural concerns. How are we to defend the intrinsic value of complex literature, difficult music, less-than-immediately-accessible art, if exactly the same intrinsic value can be induced by television, tractor pulls, or acid rock?

There is, I believe, a degree of (perhaps class-based) cultural snobbism in these reactions. That need not be the whole story, however. The fear that hedonism would devastate the cultural realm suggests a revealing lack of confidence in our preferred activities. Surely they have provided enormous delight; were that not so, were we forced to defend them as bitter medicine for the soul, we should be led to question whether they are sources of intrinsic value.

As for all those "other activities" across the fence, there may be the suspicion that those engaging in them really are having all the fun, so fun (pleasure) had better not be the intrinsically good. But are they having all that much pleasure? We should be cautiously empirical here. Perhaps Thoreau was on to something in suggesting that the mass of men [people] lead lives of quiet desperation. And then again, perhaps not. It is at least premature to conclude that we cannot make a hedonic case for high culture or (perhaps) against some popular activities. What we should not expect is that at any time all people could gain pleasure from, and thereby realize intrinsic value from, the same activities. It is, I believe, no great loss if we no longer have a guaranteed, a priori basis for saying that *our* activities produce intrinsic value and *theirs* do not.

IS PLEASURE EPIPHENOMENAL?

Pleasure—the intrinsically good—is in the realm of qualia, of intrinsic qualities of conscious experience. Much of contemporary philosophy of mind would either deny that there are such qualities or would, perhaps, just hope that they would go away. If naturalizing the mental requires showing that all mental properties are respectably material, then intrinsic qualities of color, or sound, or pleasure and pain are properties we could as well do without.

One can argue in the other direction, however. If qualities are really there and must figure in any correct description of our experience, then they part of the natural world and should be included in any naturalistic account of the mind. If that defeats a *reductive* naturalism, so be it.

But might phenomenal qualities be purely *epiphenomenal*, playing no causal role in our behavior? This is a possibility I cannot dismiss a priori. Which causal roles we can (plausibly) assign to which properties is a matter of high theory, and perhaps of theory yet to come, though I am also inclined (as a realist) to say that the causal roles of sundry properties and objects have been determined by nature.

I have admittedly danced all around this question in my appeal to neuropsychological evidence concerning the causal role of Reward Events. Do the neuropsychological events play their roles qua pleasure or only (for example) qua dopamine circuitry? I have no easy answers to this fundamental question.

As a realist I must continue to admit the possibility that intrinsic phenomenal qualities play no causal role. If that is the truth of the matter, then my theory of intrinsic value would be somewhat schizophrenic. On the one hand, I do not believe this result would alter the intrinsic goodness of pleasure. Such goodness is—I repeat as a litany—an intrinsic property that is not constituted by any further relations (including causal relations) in which such a property may stand. On the other hand, an epiphenomenal property would no longer meet my own constraint of plausibility; it would no longer, in any causally meaningful sense, be what we pursued, or desired, or were motivated to obtain. Intrinsic value could still be a real, natural property, but it would no longer do any work.

In a curious way, I do not find this possibility totally threatening. Perhaps it is a mistake to connect intrinsic value with work at all. Perhaps the proper locus of intrinsic value is in a realm of pure delight, and to insist otherwise is a remnant puritan scruple. (Santayana defended something like this position; value is in the Realm of Essence, which is totally epiphenomenal, and to have it otherwise is a corruption of spirit.)

Nevertheless, such a loss of causal role would undercut many of my empirically based arguments and would make my theory, by my own criteria, rather anemically naturalistic. I will for now take heart in those theories that do appeal to psychological properties, including properties of reward and pleasure.

VALUE, EXPERIENCE, AND INTUITIONS

There may remain a suspicion that—epiphenomenal or no—confining intrinsic value to the realm of the phenomenal makes intrinsic value altogether too superficial. Surely value should run deeper than that. But in what sense is the phenomenal superficial or on the surface of things or not deep? To counter spatial metaphors with temporal, why not see the phenomenal as a late biological flowering of complex organisms?

But neither the higher nor the later is thereby more valuable. What I am inclined to say is that any intrinsic value that was so theoretical that it could not appear within conscious experience could not be the value that makes a difference to the quality of sentient lives.

The possibility remains of constituting value from some complex, relational psychological properties. I have already discussed relational-property theories, but I should say something more about the methodology that would appeal to our intuitions about what we value or really want for our lives.[2]

I would agree that a theory that made intrinsic value a property (or kind of property) that no one could recognize as good would be a theory run mad. While I think we should be prepared to be surprised, perhaps radically surprised, by plausible theories about the causes of things and thus of how we work, I do not believe that a theory of intrinsic value can be radical in that way. If value were that hidden from the view of ordinary creatures, even if it were *true of* their lives, it would not be the value that matters *in* the lives of any of us. In that sense intrinsic value must be on the surface of experience, and that is precisely where the phenomenal is.

Despite that concession, however, I believe we can discount or reinterpret many of the intuitions appealed to in value theory, particularly if we can explain them in a way that leaves intrinsic value accessible in a naturalistically plausible way. That has been my approach in using the Reward Event Theory to explain the central role of Reward Events while at the same time explaining why it may not seem that way to our reflective self-understanding.

HEDONISM AND TEMPERAMENT

If one aims to develop a philosophical theory naturalistically, in the sense of operating within empirical constraints and making the theory vulnerable to empirical evidence, then one can be genuinely surprised at where the theory comes out.

I have been surprised to discover myself defending a version of hedonism. It is not a theory to which I am temperamentally suited, at least as such a theory is ordinarily understood. I have what I like to call a strong Thoreauvian streak, though I suspect it could as accurately be described as puritan scruples or even as downright priggishness. I have a real taste for austerity and simplicity, for a low consumption profile (which I can see as ecologically benign); indeed, were it not for the luck of being married to a gourmet cook, I might long since have lapsed into a beans-and-water diet. Add to this a preference for order that can border on the compulsive (today is Friday so I *must* do the laundry, clean the house, mow the lawn, and write letters) and you have a cast of mind that is fairly opaque to the Dionysian dimensions of life.

The point of this brief autobiographical digression is to note that in the past, this cast of mind generated strong intuitions that sundry activities described as highly pleasurable by their participants could not really have intrinsic value. It also generated strong positive intuitions that strenuous hiking on Mt. Rainier had intrinsic value in a way closed to all those who only drove to the major sights, and even that a theory of value must accommodate the possibility that Mt. Rainier itself had intrinsic value.

A combination of suggestive empirical evidence (the neuropsychological), philosophical naturalism (which was bound to question there being intrinsic value out there), and a general skepticism has led me to discount these intuitions, particularly because I believe my theory can explain them while not justifying them. Such a reassessment can be assisted by more chance associations. I have long admired Hume, and so his defense of the intrinsic value (pleasure) available from alcohol put that source of pleasure in quite a new light.

This theoretical understanding does not change my temperament; I will continue to seek pleasure from strenuous hiking rather than at the nearest pub. What is theoretically important, however, is that my theory provides a way of understanding what is going on when creatures find intrinsic value in widely various activities. And if the neuropsychology is correct, what is going on is surprising, counterintuitive, and bound to generate misunderstanding about what we really want.

I also find supporting evidence not only in the great variety across lives but also within lives over time. What we find valuable at one time of life ceases to delight, and (if we are lucky) new forms of delight develop. I think it is not plausible to explain these phenomena by saying that the phenomena out there (in the sense of not being within conscious experience) have changed their intrinsic value. For some, it will be plausible to say that the value is out there and that in changing *we* have lost (or gained?) the ability to apprehend the value. I find explanations of such apprehension epistemologically unpersuasive, however, and they also tend to be either question-begging or ungenerous in their ascription of such abilities, which are often limited to the cognitively sophisticated or to those who share "our" intuitions.

Still, if hedonism is true, both as a theory of motivation and as a theory of intrinsic value, this is a surprising truth. And, yet, if we are natural, contingent creatures who are the products of evolution, with all its quirks, perhaps it is not surprising that intrinsic value should turn up in all sorts of curious contexts. In addition, creatures have to be motivated some way, and perhaps it is the greatest luck of all that for some creatures that which is intrinsically motivating is also intrinsically valuable. Here nature has been generous, and not only to us.

NOTES

Chapter 1

1. "Externalist" theories of knowledge claim that in order for S to know, for example, that some object a has property P, there must be an appropriate link between internal states of S and the object a and the property P, but that S need not know that there is such a link. In brief, some of the foundations of knowledge need not be known. Correspondingly, the justifiability of a belief depends on more than a believer's total doxastic state; it depends on contingent facts such as, for example, the reliability of one's cognitive processes in producing true beliefs. By contrast, "internalist" theories insist that knowledge (or at least justification) must be based on internal states of the believer so that "we can vary everything about the situation other than the internal states without affecting which beliefs are justifiable" (Pollock 1986, 22). Pollock provides a detailed discussion of varieties of internalist and externalist theories.

2. I originally developed this argument in the context of a fairly detailed discussion (Morillo 1984) of the theory of Dretske (1981). Much of that discussion has been eliminated here, but I wish to emphasize how much my own ideas were formed as a response to Dretske's theory.

3. This modifies my original claim (Morillo 1984) that truth is the only virtue of a single belief. If the virtue of a belief has to do with, for example, its contribution to successful action, then relevance to current aims is also needed. And when one considers the virtues of whole theories, the story is even more complicated. (See Kitcher 1992 for a lucid survey of the issues.) Nevertheless, a single belief, qua belief, has as its virtue truth.

4. Of course, if one were a "true believer" in a sufficiently high percentage of one's beliefs, one might conclude either that one is thereby a knower or that being a knower isn't all that important.

5. See particularly the writings of Stephen Jay Gould, which undercut the popular mythology of Nature always producing the Perfectly Adapted Creature for all circumstances.

6. I would also note—looking ahead—that in my theory of intrinsic value, such value can turn up in very disreputable company, including the company of epistemically disreputable beliefs. The good is not bound to truth and wisdom. Of course, that a false belief gives us pleasure does nothing to make it true; nothing can make a false belief true. That we gain pleasure arrived at by an unreliable method has more serious implication for our long-term economy, but even that does not undercut the intrinsic value produced by that belief.

7. For an excellent discussion of the varying roles of ecological assumptions and constraints and internal mechanisms, see Bogdan 1994. Bogdan, quite properly, stresses the increasing role in sophisticated cognizers of internal mechanisms that allow for swift adaptation to changing circumstances.

8. Despite my fundamental theoretical disagreement with Armon-Jones with respect to the nature of feeling, there is much at the midlevel of her theory that I find very congenial. Her arguments are well-grounded in the psychological evidence, though she puts less emphasis on the neuropsychological evidence than do I. She provides a very persuasive argument for the role of ideology and rationalization in the folk-psychological characterizations of emotions; such characterizations, she concludes, are often quite misleading if taken as adequate accounts of what is really going on, causally, when affect plays a role in our psychology, and can lead us to overlook the central causal role of feeling. I will be presenting my own arguments for how cognitive assumptions and ideology can mislead us, not only about what is going on psychologically, but also about the nature of intrinsic value.

Chapter 2

1. This chapter combines material from Morillo 1990, 1992.

2. These events are central to my theory of motivation and of value; I shall hereafter capitalize this label in order to emphasize their theoretical role, and the fact that I interpret such events in ways that would not be accepted by many psychologists or philosophers.

3. In private correspondence, Rachels has expressed continuing support for his argument; Feinberg, also in private correspondence, has stated that he is not committed to the argument, which is included in his introductory text purely for pedagogical purposes.

4. For historical accuracy, it should be noted that Hull developed a *"drive* theory of reinforcement and learning in which bodily need led to drive, which then led to new learned behavior to correct the need and reduce the drive, thus reinforcing the learning" (Stellar and Stellar 1985, 23). This does seem to give a primary role to internal conditions in the organism, but these are internal physiological conditions, and to the degree that the psychological terms, e.g., drive and reinforcement, are defined operationally in terms of patterns of behavior, it is still in the spirit of behaviorism.

5. It will be clear, from many of the quotations I will be using, that these experiments raise significant ethical issues concerning our treatment of nonhuman animals. I have read the literature with an uneasy combination of intellectual fascination and ethical concern.

6. There is already considerable evidence that this is not true of all cases of learning, that in many if not most creatures, there is considerable latent learning—associations learned in the absence of any reward. Of course, the experiments were considering the traditional rewards of food, water, etc.; it is much more difficult to control for the absence of a kind of brain event. But there may be deep differences between motivated and unmotivated learning, and since my concern is with motivation, we can let that pass. See Stellar and Stellar 1985: "Thus, even if motivation and reward are not necessary conditions for all classical conditioning, they often accompany it. In operant conditioning, of course, motivation and reward are clearly two conditions that must prevail if the law of effect is to apply" (18).

7. Keep in mind that we are bracketing analogous processes of negative conditioning through aversive stimuli.

8. See the comment by Wise (1982): "A reinforcer is defined by its ability to serve in response acquisition; food is defined as reinforcing to hungry animals because if food is presented after some arbitrary act of the animal, it will increase the frequency of emission of that act when the animal is hungry again" (40).

9. There is abundant evidence for this. There is also evidence that self-administration of cocaine and other drugs operates through a similar dopamine-based brain circuit. See Stellar and Stellar 1985; Wise 1982; Engel et al. 1987.

10. See Wise (1982) on effects of dopamine blockers on operant conditioning with food reward. A recent report in *Scientific American* (November 1988) outlines a theory of anorexia that is in the spirit of the Reward Event Theory. "One specific theory, advocated by Mary Ann Marrazzi and Elliot D. Luby of the Wayne State University School of Medicine, suggests that anorexia is perpetuated by an addiction to starvation. In particular, they say, prolonged starvation is thought to elicit the release of certain endogenous (self-produced) narcotic-like substances known as opioids. The opioids have several effects, including the slowing of the metabolism to conserve energy. They also induce an elation that could well reinforce anorexic behaviors, much as an alcoholic 'high' reinforces the desire to drink" (36).

11. With rats, there is no satiation for the ingestion of saccharine, nor is there for ESB. See also Stellar and Stellar (1985) on "stimulus-bound feeding or drinking," specifically "the observation that ESB of the lateral hypothalamus often leads to elicited feeding or drinking behavior when food or water are present (Margules & Olds, 1962; Cox, Kakloweski & Valenstein, 1969; Hoebel, 1975)" (200). Stellar and Stellar note several different interpretations of these results. One is that "natural hunger or thirst was aroused by the stimulation of a feeding or drinking circuit and that the animal acted accordingly" (200). This suggests a conceptualization of hunger as primarily a matter of brain circuitry rather than metabolic state. On the other hand, "Valenstein *et al.* (1969 [*sic*, actually 1968]) argue that somehow we have a misconception when we think of

this consummatory response as reflecting hunger elicited by ESB. Rather, they suggest that we think of the ESB activating some arousal function that causes the animal to seek to execute a consummatory act" (201). In brief, there is no consensus as to which aspects of a complex internal state should receive the hunger label.

12. We might speculate on a similar causal explanation for the human phenomenon of pica, a craving for nonnutritive substances such as chalk and ashes. Note the interesting conceptual choice made by *Webster's New Collegiate Dictionary* (1949), which defines 'pica' as "craving for unnatural *food*. . ." (637, my emphasis).

13. There would be even further justification for this move if one wished to define key motivational states, such as hunger, in terms of those roles that no doubt explain their evolution.

14. See Stellar and Stellar (1985): "One difference is the reliance of most natural rewards on a motivational state such as hunger or thirst. In ESB self-stimulation, no steady motivational state is present" (199).

15. The insight intended here is a kind of rational insight, to be discussed below. In quite another sense, it is no doubt the case that evolutionary theory provides important insights into why natural creatures have standard desires or motivations for food, sex, and so on. No creature lacking these motivations could survive or contribute to evolution.

16. The contrast is incomplete. Even if no external goal is ever intrinsically rewarding, or ever becomes functionally autonomous with respect to the Reward Event, we would still need to distinguish among:

1. Innate Direct Goals: external goals that are innately directly rewarding.
2. Innate Derivative Goals: external goals that, innately, are rewarding only through a wired-in association (contingent connection) with some external goal that is innately directly rewarding.
3. Learned Direct Goals: external goals that are not innately rewarding in either sense one or two, but where experienced associations with goals of type one, type two, or (perhaps) type four, produce new contingent connections in the brain such that the goal becomes directly rewarding, and at that point becomes functionally autonomous with respect to other external goals.
4. Learned Derivative Goals: external goals that are not innately rewarding in either sense one or two, but that by learned association with external goals of either type one or type two come to be pursued, but remain functionally dependent on the type one and type two goals.
5. Cognitively Derived Direct Goals: external goals that are not innately rewarding in either sense one or two, but where cognitive development (new beliefs, knowledge, concepts, etc.), independent of any association with any other rewards, produces new contingent connections in the brain such that the goal becomes directly rewarding.
6. Cognitively Derived Derivative Goals: external goals that are not innately rewarding in either sense one or two, but where learned beliefs about how that goal can lead to or help produce, ultimately, an external goal that is directly rewarding, cause it to become a goal.

7. Cognitively/Affectively Derived Derivative Goals: external goals that are not innately rewarding in either sense one or two, but where learned beliefs about how that goal can lead to or help produce, ultimately, some external goal that is directly rewarding, plus some thought of or envisagement of the directly rewarding goal, which thought or envisagement is itself directly rewarding, combine to cause something to become a goal.

8. Noncognitively Derived Direct Goals: external goals that are not innately rewarding in either sense one or two, but where contingent changes that are neither cognitive nor involve associations with any other rewards (rewiring through brain surgery?) produce new contingent connections in the brain such that the goal becomes directly rewarding.

Which of these possibilities has any actual instances is one of the things one hopes further empirical research will determine. Depending on the results, we would have rather different versions of RET, which can thus be seen to be a quite general kind of theory, which opens up a good deal of empirical space.

Chapter 3

1. Such questions were asked by my colleagues, Norton Nelkin and Ed Johnson; I have been driven to pursue these questions by their challenging criticisms.

2. Nelkin has argued for several distinct types of consciousness, and in that context has argued for the possibility of unfelt sensations (1987, 1989a, 1989b, 1993a, 1993b).

3. See Strawson's whimsical speculation about why some philosophers deny the existence of phenomenal experience, 1994, 317.

4. Some probing questions by Richard Brandt (in private correspondence) led me to try to say more about these complex empirical issues.

Chapter 4

1. See the entry on "Value and Valuation" by William Frankena in the *Encyclopedia of Philosophy* (1965), for a survey of usages.

2. This is not a very rigorous specification of naturalism, but I hope it captures the spirit of many contemporary philosophical theories (e.g., theories of perception and cognition) that are making increasing use of scientific theories. The lines are once again blurring between philosophy and the sciences, to the benefit of both.

3. Has there ever been such a theory? The closest example I can think of would be a theory that claimed that God is the sole intrinsic good and that our natures are such, because of Original Sin, that we are incapable on our own of being motivated to pursue that good, but are rather motivated to pursue evil. But

even this theory would maintain that with grace we can become capable of pursuing the good. So even such a "supernaturalistic" theory could meet the plausibility constraint; I am mainly concerned with the implication of the constraint for naturalistic theories.

4. The same on some level of description, such as "Desired by some subject S, under constraints C." Different S's might be seen as constituting different properties.

5. Note that for RET, even the standard primary rewards such as food, water, and sex, are functionally dependent on Reward Events.

6. It is surprising that Brandt should argue this way, since elsewhere in his book he argues persuasively for a "satisfaction or happiness" theory as opposed to a "desire theory" of welfare. However, recent personal correspondence with Brandt has convinced me that our deepest disagreement is not about the causal role of satisfaction ("gratifications"), or about the primacy of satisfaction over preference, but about the theoretical interpretation of satisfaction or pleasure.

7. This is on the assumption that such practical reasoning is a consciously monitored phenomenon. A version of RET that postulated nonconscious expectations of Reward Events would give deliberation a wider role.

8. Compare Millikan 1984, whose naturalistic theory of cognition and representation is grounded in evolutionary claims about how those mechanisms are supposed to work.

9. See, for example., B. Angrist 1987 (in Engel et al. 1987), especially 111; see also the other articles in this collection, as well as descriptions in Stellar and Stellar 1985.

10. As one example, note the following strong statements by a researcher dealing with drug addiction: "For anyone with a biological education it is clear that the development of dependence is based on pleasurable experiences via the brain reward systems. . . . The experience of pleasure—or a marked reduction of pain and discomfort—is the basis for an interest in drug consumption. . . . The pleasure-producing properties of the drug are thus the basic element" (Bejerot 1987, 177). Other researchers may disagree with Bejerot, but his claims would generally be taken to be empirical, causal claims, not conceptual truths. See also my discussion of the Wise and Bozarth theory of addiction in chapter 2.

11. The extreme, unfocused depression in the bipolar syndrome (manic/depressive) is an example of pure awfulness; those who undergo these experiences often characterize them as worse than any physical pain.

12. Or at least not consciously guided. A theory might extend the concept of guidance to creatures who do not consciously deliberate about what they ought to do. See Bogdan 1994.

13. But we should note the following phenomenon, reported by Porrino (1987, 53):

> In fact, rats learn to escape response-independent presentation of electrical brain stimulation for which they had previously worked. In order to isolate the neural circuits associated with the contingent presentation of electrical stimulation to the VTA [Ventral Tegmental Area] that are, therefore, directly related to reinforcement, we compared rates of glucose utilization in three groups of rats: (a) animals self-stimulating to the VTA; (b) animals receiving experimenter-administered

electrical stimulation (EAS) to the VTA at rates and parameters for which they had previously self-stimulated; and (c) animals receiving no stimulation. Both the ICSS and the EAS groups showed a similar pattern of metabolic activation, as assessed by changes in LCGU [Local Cerebral Glucose Utilization], at the stimulation site and in the direct rostral and caudal projection fibers in the medial forebrain bundle and pontine gray. . . . The pattern of alterations in local metabolic rates in ICSS and EAS animals were divergent, however, in the terminal fields of the VTA. There were extensive changes in glucose utilization in the ICSS animals that were not present in the EAS group.

Neo-Aristotelians might take heart at the possibility of a biological bias toward activity as a source of Reward Events; such a bias would make considerable evolutionary sense. My colleague, Ed Johnson, has suggested a label for such an Aristotelian rodent—Autonomouse. In contemporary settings, the activity may be rather minimal, however—bar pressing, smoking crack, or what have you.

14. A caution here. To the degree we can speculate (no doubt anthropomorphically) about the state of mind of a rat, it is more likely that the rat, unaware of the causal activity of the electrodes in his brain, or indeed that he has a brain at all, would "on reflection" characterize his condition as one in which he is committed to, for example, bar pressing for its own sake. If the electrodes are disconnected, so bar pressing no longer produces ESB, the rat might after a while note with Wordsworthian sorrow that the magic had departed from those joyous activities of earlier times, and perhaps decide that *he* had failed.

15. The story I have told here, if defensible, provides some of my reasons for rejecting Brandt's (1979) motivational theoretical-construct theory of pleasure. We should not define pleasure or an intrinsically rewarding event in terms of motivation to do anything; it is a contingent fact that these events do (in most cases) cause motivation. There is perhaps a shade too much of the work ethic in Brandt's definitions.

16. To balance the books a bit on the ideology of our second story, I would recommend that one read the section on the Imam who would "stop time," in Rushdie 1989, 205-215. It is not an attractive picture.

Chapter 5

1. Once again I must emphasize that I am presenting only a half theory; a full theory would have to bring in negative hedonic tone, and a final balance sheet would have to weigh the positive against the negative.

2. In a later paper, Brandt (1984), in an overall defense of a "happiness" theory of "benefit," which is close to what he calls "pure hedonism," develops a "kind of desire theory" of intrinsic value. This theory, along with his "motivational" theory of pleasure, involves him in many of the same difficulties and obscurities that he (correctly) attributes to preference theories. He tries to avoid the problems by specifying that "to be an intrinsic good, the desire for something must be just prior to the event of its satisfaction (along with gladness during and after the event)" (38), but these temporal limitations seem arbitrary.

3. That is, those capable of distinct experiences of affect, and that share a Reward- (Aversion-) Event psychology.

4. Briefly, the issue is whether to include in a utilitarian balance sheet, not only the positive or negative experiences of an individual, but also the positive or negative experiences of others when they contemplate that individual's experiences. Does my pleasant experience count more if others are pleased that I have it?

5. See the writings of Stephen Jay Gould, particularly 1989.

6. Some of the experiments of Wise, using dopamine-blockers on rats, suggest such results. And the anhedonia and failure of motivation of extreme depression may be a very sad natural experiment with the same implications.

7. For an excellent discussion of the issues involved in evaluating the lives of other species, see the paper by my colleague Ed Johnson (1989).

8. Note that we can derive positive affect from contemplation of kinds of lives that do not share a psychology of affect, and thus that do not have experiences with intrinsic value. This may help keep such species in the picture and ameliorate otherwise discomforting implications of RET with respect to our dealings with much of nature.

9. From "Nineteen Hundred and Nineteen," in Finneran 1990, 208.

10. From the final sentence of *The Origin of Species*.

11. In Boswell, *Life of Dr. Johnson*, vol. 2, 117, my emphasis.

Chapter 6

1. See Nagel 1986, 153-54; Parfit 1984, 143; Gauthier 1986, 46-59.

2. To say that one is simply locating the pain does not entail that this locus is a "mere receptacle" in a morally pejorative sense. The pain is an episode in the life of the *subject* of the pain; that an individual creature is capable of experiencing pleasure or pain is, on any sane moral theory, morally significant. It takes a further ethical argument, however, to establish how some other individual should respond to this significance.

3. For replies to challenges to any too-demanding morality, see Morillo 1976, 1977b, 1985.

4. In extending the concept of belief in this noncognitivist way, Gibbard is developing a ground for ethical theory that most decidedly will not be a variant of the currently popular moral realism, which does involve truth-commitment beliefs. (See Sturgeon, 1984, 1986a, 1986b, 1987; Brink, 1989; Railton, 1986.)

5. There is a further theoretical/terminological issue concerning the naturalization of norms. I have implicitly agreed with Gibbard that norms are best seen as social devices, but this could be questioned. If any social control device must operate through individual psychological mechanisms, the internal devices might be seen as the fundamental normative mechanisms, which could operate not only in social creatures but also in solitary creatures that had no need for any social coordination. These mechanisms would be basic yes/no or accept/reject devices. (It would be a further theoretical issue as to whether, in at least some creatures, such an accept/reject device is based on internal brain events that are,

respectively, instances of positive and negative hedonic tone. This is the theory I have been defending.) Insofar as this mechanism valences the world, and in that sense tells the creature "Do this," or "Don't do that," it could be seen as the basis of fundamental individual norms, which are prior to and presupposed by any internalization of social norms.

I do not have strong convictions about this terminological issue. There are three distinct sorts of processes we need to consider: the internal psychological devices that could be common to both social and solitary creatures; the processes of internalization, in which a social creature takes on specific rules of action as a result of either an evolutionary wiring in or of responses to various pressures from conspecifics; and those full-blown human practices that involve language, discussion, and even explicit instruction in the rules. I am inclined to split the difference between those who would use the term 'norms' for all these processes and those who would restrict it to human practices. This is the middle-ground that Gibbard also accepts, as he extends norms to some nonhuman creatures, but only to social creatures in need of some coordination device.

6. There is the further issue as to whether a completely naturalized, and properly cognitive, conception of having reasons or being rational is the appropriate conception on which to ground all ethical norms. Being strategically rational (having means-ends rationality) may be an indispensable tool for getting along in the world, but when it comes to our ultimate ends, or to our basic ethical norms, is it clear that the appropriate ur-norm is, Above all, be rational? If such rationality is genuinely cognitive, then it may leave out (as I would argue) any intrinsic value, and that would be a serious omission in any ethical theory.

Chapter 7

1. Quoted in A. Baier 1991, 204. I recommend Baier's entire discussion of Hume's hedonism and his attacks on "puritan scruples about the pleasurable."

2. See Brink 1989 for a sophisticated use, by a value realist, of such a methodology.

BIBLIOGRAPHY

Ailoy, L. B. and A. H. Ahrens. 1987. Depression and pessimism for the future: biased use of statistically relevant information in predictions for self versus others. *Journal of Personality and Social Psychology* 52: 366-378.

Angrist, B. 1987. Clinical effects of central nervous stimulants: a selective update. In Engel et al., 109-127.

Armon-Jones, C. 1991. *Varieties of Affect*. Toronto: University of Toronto Press.

Baier, A. 1991. *A Progress of Sentiments: Reflections on Hume's Treatise.* Cambridge, MA: Harvard University Press.

Bejerot, N. 1987. Addiction: clinical and theoretical consideration. In Engel et al., 177-180.

Bogdan, R. 1994. *Grounds for Cognition: How Goal-Guided Behavior Shapes the Mind.* Hillsdale, NJ: Lawrence Erlbaum Associates, Publishers.

Brandt, R. 1979. *A Theory of the Good and the Right.* New York: Oxford University Press.

_____. 1989. Fairness to happiness. *Social Theory and Practice* 15: 33-58.

_____. 1992. The rational criticism of preferences. Unpublished manuscript.

Brink, D. 1989. *Moral Realism and the Foundation of Ethics.* New York: Cambridge University Press.

Brown, J. D. 1984. Effects on induced mood on causal attributions for success and failure. *Motivation and Emotion* 8: 343-353.

Cohen, S. 1984. Justification and truth. *Philosophical Studies* 46: 279-296.

Copp, D. and D Zimmerman, eds. 1985. c.1984. *Morality, Reason and Truth.* Totowa, NJ: Rowman & Allanheld.

Cox, V., J. Kakolewski and E. Valenstein. 1969. Inhibition of eating and drinking following hypothalamic stimulation in the rat. *Journal of Comparative and Physiological Psychology* 68: 530-535.

177

Darwin, C. 1859. *The Origin of Species*. Many editions.

de Sousa, R. 1987. *The Rationality of Emotion*. Cambridge, MA: MIT Press.

Dethier, V. G. 1976. *The Hungry Fly*. Cambridge, MA: Harvard University Press.

Dretske, F. 1981. *Knowledge and the Flow of Information*. Cambridge, MA: MIT Press.

Edelman, G. 1987. *Neural Darwinism*. New York: Basic Books.

———. 1989. *The Remembered Present*. New York: Basic Books.

———. 1992. *Bright Air, Brilliant Fire: On the Matter of the Mind*. New York: Basic Books.

Edwards, P., ed. 1967. *The Encyclopedia of Philosophy*. New York: Macmillan.

Edwards, R. 1979. *Pleasures and Pains: A Theory of Qualitative Hedonism*. Ithaca, NY: Cornell University Press.

Engel, J., L. Oreland, D. Ingvar, B. A Pernow, S. Rössner, and L. Pellborn. 1987. *Brain Reward Systems and Abuse*. New York: Raven Press.

Facey, A. B. 1981. *A Fortunate Life*. New York: Penguin Books.

Feinberg, J. 1971. Psychological egoism. In *Reason and Responsibility*, 2d ed., edited by Feinberg, 489-500. Encino, CA: Dickenson.

Findlay, J. N. 1961. *Values and Intentions*. New York: Macmillan.

Finneran, R., ed. 1990. *W.B. Yeats: The Poems, Revised*. New York: Macmillan.

Frankena, W. K. 1939. The naturalistic fallacy. *Mind* 48: 103-114.

———. 1967. Value and valuation. In Edwards 1967, vol. 8, 229-232.

Gallistel, C. R., J. R. Stellar, and E. Bubis. 1974. Parametric analysis of brain stimulation reward in the rat: I. The transient process and the memory-containing process. *Journal of Comparative Physiological Psychology* 87: 848-859.

Gauthier, D. 1986. *Morals By Agreement*. New York: Oxford University Press.

Gibbard, A. 1990. *Wise Choices, Apt Feelings: A Theory of Normative Judgment*. Cambridge, MA: Harvard University Press.

Gillespie, N., ed. 1986. *Moral Realism: Proceedings of the 1985 Spindel Conference. The Southern Journal of Philosophy, Supplement 24*.

Gilligan, S. G. and G. H. Bower. 1984. Cognitive consequences of emotional arousal. In *Emotion, cognition and Behavior*, edited by C. I. Izard, J. Kagan, and R. Zajonc, 547-588. New York: Cambridge University Press.

Gloor, P., A. Olivier, L. Quesney, F. Andermann, and S. Horowitz. 1982. The role of the limbic system in experimental phenomena of temporal lobe epilepsy. *Annals of Neurology* 12: 140.

Goldman, A. 1976. Discrimination and perceptual knowledge. *The Journal of Philosophy* 73: 771-791.

Gould, S. J. 1989. *Wonderful Life: The Burgess Shale and the Nature of History*. New York: W. W. Norton.

Gray, T. and R. A. Wise. 1980. Effects of pimozide on lever-pressing behavior maintained on an intermittent reinforcement schedule. *Pharmacology, Biochemistry and Behavior* 12: 931-935.

Griffin, J. 1986. *Well-Being: Its Meaning, Measurement and Moral Importance*. New York: Oxford University Press.

Grill, H. J. and R. Norgren. 1978a. The taste reactivity test. 2. Mimetic responses in gustatory stimuli in chronic thalamic and chronic decerebrate rats. *Brain Research* 143: 281-297.

_____. 1978b. Chronically decerebrate rats demonstrate satiation but not bait shyness. *Science* 201: 267-269.

Gunne, L. M., E. Änggar, and L. E. Jönsson. 1972. Clinical trials with amphetamine-blocking drugs. *Psychiatria Neurologia Neurochirurgia* 75: 225-226.

Heath, R. G., ed. 1964. *The Role of Pleasure in Behavior.* New York: Harper & Row.

Heller, W. 1990. The neuropsychology of emotion: developmental patterns and implications for psychopathology. In Stein et al., 167-211.

Hoebel, B. G. 1975. Brain reward and aversion systems in the control of feeding and sexual behavior. In *Nebraska Symposium on Motivation*, edited by J. Cole and T. Sonderegger,49-112. Lincoln: University of Nebraska Press.

Houk, J. C., J .L. Davis, and D. G. Beiser, eds. 1994. *Models of Information Processing in the Basal Ganglia.* Cambridge, MA: The MIT Press.

Hume, D. 1978. *A Treatise of Human Nature*, 2d ed., edited by L. A. Selby-Bigge and P. H. Nidditch. Oxford: Oxford University Press.

Isen, A. M., K. A. Daubman, and G. P. Nowicki 1987. Positive affect facilitates creative problem solving. *Journal of Personality and Social Psychology* 52: 1122-1131.

Johnson, E. 1989. Life, death, and animals. In Regan and Singer, 139-149.

Johnson, M. H. and P. A. Magaro. 1987. Effects of mood and severity on memory processes in depression and mania. *Psychological Bulletin* 10: 28-40.

Jönsson, L., E. Änggard, and L. Gunne. 1971. Blockade of intravenous amphetamine euphoria in man. *Clinical Pharmacology and Therapy* 12: 889-896.

Katz, L. 1982. Hedonic arousal, memory, and motivation. Commentary on Wise. *Behavioral and Brain Sciences* 5: 60.

Kitcher, P. 1992. The naturalists return. *The Philosophical Review* 101: 53-114.

Kundera, M. 1985. *The Unbearable Lightness of Being.* New York: Harper & Row.

Lettvin, J. Y., A. Maturana, W. S. McCulloch, and W. H. Pitts. 1959. What the frog's eye tells the frog's brain. *Proceedings of the Institute of Radio Engineers* 47: 1940-1951.

Mackie, J. 1977. *Ethics: Inventing Right and Wrong.* New York: Penguin Books.

Madigan, R. J. and A. K. Bollenbach. 1986. The effects of induced mood on irrational thought and views of the world. *Cognitive Therapy and Research* 10: 547-562.

Mandler, G. 1984. *Mind and Body: Psychology of Emotion and Stress.* New York: Norton.

_____. 1990. A constructivist theory of emotion. In Stein et al., 21-43.

Margules, D. L. and J. Olds. 1962. Identical "feeding" and "rewarding" systems in the lateral hypothalamus of rats. *Science* 135: 374-375.

Mendola, J. 1990. An ordinal modification of classical utilitarianism. *Erkenntnis* 33: 73-88.

Milgram, S. 1974. *Obedience to Authority: An Experimental View.* New York: Harper & Row.

Mill, J. S. 1861. *Utilitarianism.* Many editions.

Millikan, R. 1984. *Language, Thought, and Other Biological Categories.* Cambridge, MA: MIT Press.

Moore, G. E. 1903. *Principia Ethica*. Cambridge: Cambridge University Press.

Morillo, C. R. 1976. As sure as shooting. *Philosophy* 51: 80-89.

_____. 1977a. The logic of arguments from contingency. *Philosophy and Phenomenological Research* 37: 407-417.

_____. 1977b. Doing, refraining, and the strenuousness of morality. *American Philosophical Quarterly* 14: 29-39.

_____. 1984. Epistemic luck, naturalistic epistemology, and the ecology of knowledge: or what the frog should have told Dretske. *Philosophical Studies* 46: 109-129.

_____. 1985. Defining duties and constructing morality: comments on Narveson. *Tulane Studies in Philosophy* 31: 58-66.

_____. 1992. Reward event systems: reconceptualizing the explanatory role of motivation, desire and pleasure. *Philosophical Psychology* 5: 7-32.

Nagel, T. 1970. *The Possibility of Altruism*. New York: Oxford University Press.

_____. 1986. *The View From Nowhere*. New York: Oxford University Press.

Nelkin, N. 1986. Pains and pain sensation. *The Journal of Philosophy* 83: 129-148.

_____. 1987. What is it like to be a person? *Mind and Language* 2: 220-241.

_____. 1989a. Propositional attitudes and consciousness. *Philosophy and Phenomenological Research* 49: 413-430.

_____. 1989b. Unconscious sensations. *Philosophical Psychology* 2, 129-141.

_____. 1993a. The connection between intentionality and consciousness. In *Consciousness*, edited by M. Davies and G. W. Humphreys, 224-239. Oxford: Basil Blackwell.

_____. 1993b. What is consciousness? *Philosophy of Science* 60: 419-434.

_____. 1994. Reconsidering pain. *Philosophical Psychology* 7: 325-343.

Olds, J. and P. Milner. 1954. Positive reinforcement produced by electrical stimulation of septal area and other regions of the rat brain. *Journal of Comparative and Physiological Psychology* 47: 419-427.

Olds, J. 1958. Self-stimulation of the brain: its use to study local effects of hunger, sex, and drugs. *Science* 127: 315-324.

Overton, D. A. 1984. State dependent learning and drug discriminations. In *Handbook of Psychopharmacology: Drugs, Neurotransmitters and Behavior* 18, edited by L. L. Iversen, S. D. Iversen, and S. H. Snyder, 59-127. New York: Plenum.

Parfitt, D. 1984. *Reasons and Persons*. New York: Oxford University Press.

Peters, R. and R. McGee. 1982. Cigarette smoking and state-dependent memory. *Psychopharmacology* 76: 232-235.

Pollock, J. L. 1986. *Contemporary Theories of Knowledge*. Totowa, NJ: Rowman & Littlefield.

Porrino, L. J. 1987. Cerebral metabolic changes associated with activation of reward systems. In Engel et al., 51-60.

Rachels, J. 1986. *The Elements of Moral Philosophy*. New York: Random House.

_____. 1989. Why animals have a right to liberty. In Regan and Singer, 122-131.

Railton, P. 1986. Moral realism. *Philosophical Review* 95: 163-207.

Regan, T. and P. Singer, eds. 1989. *Animal Rights and Human Obligations*. Englewood Cliffs, NJ: Prentice-Hall.

Rosenfield, I. 1988. *The Invention of Memory*. New York: Basic Books.

Routtenberg, A. and J. Lindy. 1965. Effects of the availability of rewarding septal and hypothalamic stimulation on bar pressing for food under conditions of deprivation. *Journal of Comparative and Physiological Psychology* 60: 158-161.

Rushdie, S. 1989. *Satanic Verses*. New York: Viking.

Schultz, W., R. Romo, T. Ljungberg, J. Mirenowicz, J. R. Holterman, and A. Dickinson. 1994. Reward-related signals carried by dopamine neurons. In Houk et al., 87-214.

Schwartz, B. 1989. *Psychology of Learning and Behavior,* 3d ed. New York: W.W. Norton & Co.

Slote, M. 1964. An empirical basis for psychological egoism. *The Journal of Philosophy* 61: 530-537.

Stein, N. L., B. Leventhal, and T. Trabaso, eds. 1990. *Psychological and Biological Approaches to Emotion*. Hillsdale, NJ: Lawrence Erlbaum Associates.

Steiner, J. E. 1973. The human gustofacial response. In *Fourth Symposium On Oral Sensation and Perception,* edited by J. F. Bosma, 254-278. Bethesda, MD: U.S. Dept. of Health, Education, and Welfare.

Stellar, J. R. and E. Stellar 1985. *The Neurobiology of Motivation and Reward*. New York: Springer-Verlag.

Stellar, J. R. 1976. Approach-withdrawal analysis of the lateral and medial hypothalamus. Ph.D. dissertation. University of Pennsylvania.

Strawson, G. 1994. *Moral Reality*. Cambridge, MA: The MIT Press.

Sturgeon, N. 1985. Moral explanations. In Copp and Zimmerman, 49-78.

_____. 1986a. What difference does it make whether moral realism is true? In Gillespie 1986, 115-142.

_____. 1986b. Harman on moral explanations of natural facts. In Gillespie 1986, 69-78.

Thayer, R. E. 1987. Problem perception, optimism, and related states as a function of time of day (diurnal rhythm) and moderate exercise: two arousal systems in interaction. *Motivation and Emotion* 11: 19-36.

_____. 1989. *The Biopsychology of Mood and Arousal*. New York: Oxford University Press.

Thorndike, E. L. 1911. *Animal Intelligence*. New York: Macmillan.

Toates, F. 1980. *Animal Behavior: A Systems Approach*. New York: Wiley.

Tucker, D. M., K. Vannattaq, and R. Rothlind. 1990. Arousal and activation systems and primitive adaptive controls on cognitive priming. In Stein et al., 145-166.

Tulving, E. and D. M. Thompson 1973. Encoding specificity and retrieval processes in episodic memory. *Psychological Review* 80: 352-373.

Valenstein, E. S., V. G. Cox, and J. W. Kakolewski 1968. Modification of motivated behavior elicited by electrical stimulation of the hypothalamus. *Science* 159: 1119-1121.

Williams, O., ed. 1954. *The Pocket Book of Modern Verse*. New York: Pocket Books.

Wise, R.A. and M. A. Bozarth. 1982. Action of drugs of abuse on brain reward systems: an update with specific attention to opiates. *Pharmacology, Biochemistry and Behavior* 17: 239-243.

_____. 1987. A psychomotor stimulant theory of addiction. *Psychological Review* 94: 469-492.

Wise, R. A. and P.-P. Rompre. 1989. Brain dopamine and reward. *Annual Review of Psychology* 40: 191-225.

Wise, R. A. 1982. Neuroleptics and operant behavior: the anhedonia hypothesis. *Behavioral and Brain Sciences* 5: 39-52.

Wright, W. F. and G. H. Bower. 1981. Mood effects on subjective probability assessments. Unpublished manuscript as described in Gilligan and Bower, 1984.

INDEX

ABOUT THE AUTHOR

Carolyn R. Morillo is professor emerita at the University of New Orleans, where she taught in the Department of Philosophy from 1960 to 1993. She has published articles on ethics, theory of knowledge, and philosophical psychology in, among others, *The Journal of Philosophy*, *Philosophical Psychology*, and *Philosophical Studies*.